Secure Commerce on the Internet

Warning and Disclaimer

Secure Commerce on the Internet

Vijay Ahuja, Ph.D.

Manager
Network Security Products
IBM Corporation

AP PROFESSIONAL
AP PROFESSIONAL is a Division of Academic Press, Inc.

Boston   San Diego   New York
London   Sydney   Tokyo   Toronto

AP PROFESSIONAL

An Imprint of ACADEMIC PRESS, INC.
A Division of HARCOURT BRACE & COMPANY

ORDERS (USA and Canada): 1-800-3131-APP or APP@ACAD.COM
AP PROFESSIONAL Orders: 6277 Sea Harbor Dr., Orlando, FL 32821-9816

Europe/Middle East/Africa: 0-11-44 (0) 181-300-3322
Orders: AP PROFESSIONAL 24-28 Oval Rd., London NW1 7DX

Japan/Korea: 03-3234-3911-5
Orders: Harcourt Brace Japan, Inc., Ichibancho Central Building   22-1, Ichibancho   Chiyoda-Ku, Tokyo 102

Australia: 02-517-8999
Orders: Harcourt Brace & Co. Australia, Locked Bag 16, Marrickville, NSW 2204 Australia

Other International: (407) 345-3800
AP PROFESSIONAL Orders: 6277 Sea Harbor Dr., Orlando FL 32821-9816

Editorial: 1300 Boylston St., Chestnut Hill, MA 02167 (617)232-0500

Web: http://www.apnet.com/approfessional

United Kingdom Edition published by
ACADEMIC PRESS LIMITED
24–28 Oval Road, London NW1 7DX

Ahuja, Vijay
    Secure Commerce on the Internet / Vijay Ahuja.
        p.   cm.
    Includes bibliographical references and index.
    ISBN 0-12-045597-8 (alk. paper)
    1. Business enterprises--Computer networks--Security measures.
    2. Internet (Computer newtork) 3. World Wide Web (Information
    retrieval system) 4. Electronic Commerce. I. Title.
HD30.38.A37 1996
658.4'72--dc20

96-30881
CIP

Printed in the United States of America
    96   97   98   99   IP   9   8   7   6   5   4   3   2   1

Dedication

To my respected parents, Dr. Yog Dhyan Ahuja and Mrs. Shakuntla Ahuja, for their love, affection and moral support.

Contents

Appendices

Acknowledgements

It is always a pleasure to acknowledge the contributions and sacrifices of others in helping to complete such a major project. First, I would very much like to thank IBM Corporation and my immediate management for their encouragement and support in this endeavor. I would also like to thank the editorial staff at AP Professional, especially Gael Tannenbaum and Jacquelyn Young for their cooperation, assistance and outstanding reviews of the manuscript. A special thanks is due to my wife, Neeta, and our dear children, Vinita, Anant and Devesh, for always offering complete cooperation to my unconventional working hours during nights, weekends and holidays.

Preface

During my childhood at school, I used to see my friends' families exchange their grain for rice, and my relatives who would trade clothing for expensive china. Little did I know, I was getting my first lesson in Commerce 101.

Forty years later, cyberspace is offering another way to transact commerce. It is the next industrial frontier. The rush for gold is on, and the businesses are moving fast to take a piece of the action. Commerce on the Internet has taken off!

Along with the excitement of digital commerce, there are hurdles and challenges. The Internet must transition from a basically insecure network to an environment for trusted, reliable and private communications. The consumer and the merchant must feel at least as secure as if they were transacting business in person. The banks must be assured that banking on the Internet is no less secure than banking in person.

This book focuses on the issues, technologies and approaches for secure commerce on the Internet. It begins with a review of some major Internet break-ins followed by a description of the basic concepts of security including Internet security and firewalls. Next, we address the issues of securely transacting commerce on the Internet. We present various aspects of Web security including the X.509 certificates for users and institutions. Besides Web security, a secure commerce relies heavily on an underlying scheme to securely exchange money among various parties over the Internet. We address in detail the types of payment schemes on the Internet along with related security issues and approaches. Finally, the Appendices present a background of the TCP/IP protocols, the World Wide Web and approaches to establishing a Web site.

Our goal is to service the needs of computer professionals that have interest in understanding, establishing or supporting secure commerce on the Internet. We also hope that the book provides sufficient background to help security professionals propose approaches to secure commercial applications on the Internet. While time brings new technologies and outdates current technologies, we have attempted to focus primarily on the concepts and approaches to secure commerce on the Internet.

Introduction

"We are in the midst of a worldwide rush toward digital commerce that could ultimately result in many people's lives being conducted largely online, encompassing creation and distribution of proprietary multimedia information and other forms of intellectual property, merchandising, cashless financial transactions, and general electronic communications."

Peter G. Neumann, Risks in Digital Commerce, Communications of the ACM. Vol. 30. No. 1. January 1996. p. 154.

We live on commerce. We buy things we need with what we can offer in return. Currently, money is the means to transact the commerce. Without commerce, our society cannot function and we as individuals cannot live and enjoy our lives.

A revolution is underway, however. We are heading towards a cashless society using digital currency and online commerce over the Internet. Predictions vary on the rate at which this revolution is moving, but move it must. There are skeptics and there are optimists. But online banking is already here and I expect that it will pave the way for widespread electronic commerce.

This introduction offers a brief overview of all the topics discussed in this book. We will begin with a background of the Internet and Internet security to show how they relate to online commerce. We will then discuss commerce on the Internet and its benefits, risks, and legal implications. Each category will be discussed in its entirety in the following chapters.

Background and History

Internet

In 1969, the U.S. Department of Defense sponsored a research project to explore resource sharing among remote users. The goal was to avoid the shutdown in communications during a war by designing distributed networks that do not rely on a single centralized host. So, they adopted an approach to develop a network of computers where the control was distributed. Although a telephone network may fall victim to an atomic war, a data network could provide backup communications (Ahuja 1982).

The network was designed to transmit fixed-size packets (units of information) independently through the network. At the originating node, each message was segmented into one or more packets. Each packet carried its own destination address and followed its own route through the network. At the destination node, these packets would be reassembled into a message. For communications among heterogeneous computer systems located at remote sites, a communication protocol was also designed. This protocol, called TCP/IP (*Transmission Control Protocol/Internet Protocol*), has now become the de facto standard for the industry to transfer information. The network was called *ARPANET* after the Pentagon's Advanced Research Project Agency (ARPA) that sponsored this project. ARPANET started with four nodes in 1969. It grew to 15 nodes by July 1971 (Kahn 1971) and has now grown to several thousand nodes.

ARPANET provided the foundation for research in several areas of data networks. In the late 1970s, work had started on the TCP/IP protocols. Around 1980, the connected Internet began when DARPA (Defense Advanced Research Project Agency) started converting the ARPANET nodes to TCP/IP protocols. The transition was completed in 1983. The TCP/IP protocols were enhanced with several applications or higher-level protocols such as TELNET and FTP. Additionally, several areas of research were pursued such as packet switching, routing, congestion and flow control. As early as 1971, ARPANET research had identified the well-known reassembly and store-and-forward lockups (Kahn 1971).

The Internet has grown tremendously over the last few years. The statistics are startling. According to Network Wizards[*], the number of hosts on the Internet has grown from 1,313,000 in January 1993 to 9,472,000 in January 1996. For this survey, a host is a domain name that has an IP address and would be any computer system connected to the Internet via full or part-time, direct or dialup connections.

The Web, a part of the Internet that employs Hypertext and Common Gateway Interface (thoroughly explained in Appendix B) was introduced in 1992 and its growth started in 1993.

---

[*] This data is provided by Network Wizards and is available on the Internet at *http://www.nw.com/*.

Since then, there has been a constant growth in the number of Web sites that advertise or sell products. Internet Web pages are becoming points of sales for a growing variety of businesses. In fact, most companies have a home page on the Internet. Imagine connecting to the Web to negotiate the price of a car among several dealers. According to Bournellis (1995), the number of Web sites had grown to more than 35,000 by June 1995.

The topics of TCP/IP, Internet, World Wide Web, Web Sites, and Home Page are presented in greater detail in Appendices A, B, and C.

Internet Security

Information security dates back to the 1960s when students were assigned access to the entire computer system for fixed time intervals. When I was working on my Masters degree at the University of North Carolina in the late 1960s, I would be assigned time for the use of an IBM System/360 to execute my research programs. I would have access to most of the computing resources, although it was for a short and fixed period of time.

In the late 1960s, time-sharing facilities were introduced that allowed simultaneous computer access to more than one user. At the same time, it was realized that the system programmer should have a higher access level to computing resources than students or other users. This distinction was accomplished by assigning a unique password for the system operator, which is now called the *root password* for *system administrators*. Since then, this concept of *password* has remained with us. However, during the 1980s, we saw a networking revolution that introduced distributed access and control through the client/server networks. The system administrator as well as the users could be located at remote sites from the computer system. Now the passwords would have to be transmitted over the network. So, the earlier approach of protecting system resources from a single central point was not sufficient. A new wave of network security was dawning on the information society.

During the last two decades, network security has grown from inception to a critical part of the information world. As networks become the backbone of the industrial society, network security is becoming a prerequisite for any viable data networks.

The Internet has also become a fertile ground for schemes devised to break into data networks. Given its open and easy access for the general public, the Internet is vulnerable to more attacks from intruders than any other network. Furthermore, the Internet and its underlying TCP/IP protocols were not designed with security in mind. As a result, security is being implemented as an additional feature of the existing network, instead of a part of the original network design.

In basic terms, *network security* can be viewed as consisting of three parts. The first part verifys the identity of a user or a program before permitting access to a resource. This process is called *authentication*. The password traditionally has been used to authenticate users. The second part provides data privacy so that secret data is protected from unauthorized persons. Data privacy is often provided through the use of encryption mechanisms. The third part assures that a message was indeed sent by a specified person, and that it was not altered since it left the originator. This function is often provided through the digital signature schemes.

The preceding security services are required for various transport protocols and their applications. To begin with, consider the TCP/IP protocols for the Internet. Security services, such as authentication and privacy, are required at this level. Furthermore, TCP/IP applications, such as TELNET, FTP, and electronic mail also require authentication and privacy services. Similarly, the protocols for the Web must be protected from unauthorized access. In the last few years, a new wave of applications using the World Wide Web are emerging. Many of these applications also require security services.

However, there are several additional problems to solve. For example, we need to protect passwords during transmission over the network, and we need strong encryption schemes as well as better approaches to distribute encryption keys. Vulnerabilities exist in TCP/IP applications that must be addressed to minimize security breaches.

The topic of Internet security is presented in greater detail in Chapters 1, 2, 3, and 4.

Secure Commerce

"Can man live by Net alone?"

Steven J. Vaughan-Nichols, *Living Off the Net*, InternetWorld. June 1995. p.44

Typically, secure commerce on the Internet requires three key ingredients: the Internet along with Web services, the security services, and the commerce applications, as depicted in Figure I.1. Consider an example. Mary wants to go shopping on the Internet. Her first task is to download some (digital) cash from her bank account. So she accesses her account and withdraws some digital cash. This transaction must be securely processed.

Mary should be authenticated, the amount should be kept secret, and no one else should be able to masquerade the transaction. The commerce application, including a secure payment component, residing at the Web browser, handles the interactions with Mary and the bank. The Internet protocols must securely handle the transmission of payment information among various parties. Finally, both the commerce application and the Web protocols require security services to accomplish the transaction, as shown in Figure I.2.

Figure I.I: Components of Secure Commerce

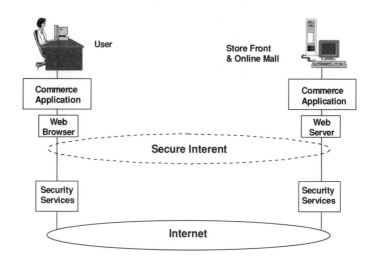

Figure 1.2: Secure Commerce on the Internet

Security Issues

Perhaps the biggest technical challenge for online commerce pertains to securing transactions over the Internet. Security has been a lingering concern for Internet users. In the following, we outline four basic types of security issues for online commerce.

The first issue relates to an electronic method to prove the identity of the consumer. This is more than authenticating the user through a password. Here, for example, the consumer needs to produce proof to establish his or her identity. It is the online version of today's driver's licence or credit card. A corresponding security issue is the possibility that someone may steal a user's proof or credentials for online identification.

The second issue pertains to secure communications among remote parties. While executing transactions, it is necessary that the data is protected and kept secret during transmission. Any successful attempts to eavesdrop on the data can compromise the privacy or secrecy of the transaction.

The third issue has to do with a secure approach for making payments. It is important that the credit card number and the date of expiration should not be accessible to anyone other than the consumer and the bank. For example, the merchant may simply require the assurance from the bank that sufficient funds are in the consumer's account for the purchase. However, the credit card information may not necessarily be divulged to the merchant. There are similar issues related to other forms of electronic payments such as electronic checks and electronic cash.

The last issue concerns security services that ensure and prove to the recipient that the message was indeed sent by the identified originator, and that the message was not modified since it left the originator. This requirement is to protect the sender and receiver from each other. In terms of network security, we call these services *nonrepudiation* and *data integrity*. Nonrepudiation requires that for an online transaction, there exists proof to establish that the buyer indeed ordered the goods and the seller actually delivered the goods. Data integrity ensures that the message was not altered since it left the originator. Finally, appropriate evidence and requisite procedures should be available to resolve any disputes or liability claims.

It has been observed by some authors that in reality, security is a relative term. Checks and charge cards are used fraudulently in day-to-day business. Businesses take steps to minimize their losses, but there is no perfect system (Ellsworth 1995). In electronic commerce, we will present approaches to enhance the security for transacting business and making payments, but again there are possible exposures such as brute-force attacks.

Given sufficient time, a brute-force attack exhausts all possibilities until the correct key is obtained to breach a system.

Commerce on Internet

Commerce on the Internet relies on the motivation of the sellers as well as the buyers. We begin by introducing the rationale for businesses to establish presence on the Internet, followed by the reasons for consumers to make online purchases. To be complete, we also include the risks and inhibitors for expanding commerce on the Internet.

Benefits to Sellers

According to Welz (1995), Forrester predicts that there will be 5.4 million Web users in 1996, growing to more than 22 million in the year 2000. It is also estimated that by that time, two-thirds of the Web users will be consumers, and the remaining one-third will be corporate and academic users. The article also quotes Forrester about the sales revenues in 1994. Out of a total of $53 billion revenue from direct sales, the online sales were only $200 million. It predicts that the revenue from online sales will grow to $4.8 billion by the year 1998.

There are several reasons for a business to establish a presence on the Internet. The first and foremost is the access to consumers. As stated, the Internet offers access to a very large number of online consumers.

Globalization is another reason to establish business presence on the Internet. Through the Internet, a business has access to customers in almost every country. It is particularly cheap when you consider the alternative of opening a shop or advertising in several countries.

Another reason for creating a business presence on the Internet is the savings in sales costs. It costs a business a considerable amount of money to establish a shop or a mall, pay the bills, salaries, and commission to their sales staff. Many of these expenses may be reduced by investing a relatively small amount to establish a home page on the Internet. These savings can in turn help reduce the costs of the goods and make them more competitive for the businesses.

Finally, businesses can provide instant updates on their merchandise. The business may insert an update on their home page that can reach online consumers instantly. Such updates may be particularly useful for selling goods or services that may expire in a very short time. For example, online updates are attractive to sell vacant seats for that night's flight to Europe or tickets for that evening's Broadway plays.

The Internet can be used by businesses for marketing, services and sales. Internet marketing includes advertising as well as providing access to information about a company. Internet services include access to a company's database for status information. For example, Federal Express and United Parcel Service provide access to their databases to check the status of packages in transit. Finally, the Internet can be used as a point of sale for merchandise, as described earlier (see Wilder 1995 for details).

Benefits to Consumers

Now, consider the criteria for consumers to shop on the Internet. As most businesses establish their home pages and store fronts on the Internet, we envision that over time consumers can access most kinds of businesses on the Internet.

Perhaps the most important consumer benefit is the savings in time. By logging onto the Internet and accessing home pages, consumers can browse through shops and merchandise from their home computers at anytime. Alternatively, in the real world, a consumer typically may spend hours for each shopping trip including travel to and from the shopping mall.

Another reason for a consumer to shop on the Internet is the convenient access to a broad variety of shops and merchandise. For example, a given shopping mall may provide clothing or other merchandise, but may not include a car dealership, an airline ticket office, or a specialty store.

Finally, a consumer may also like to shop on the Internet to compare instantly the quality and price of a given product from different stores. It can help make shopping decisions easier and faster.

Online Banking

Online banking pertains to banking services transacted using a home computer. During the 1970s, Automatic Teller Machines (ATMs) ushered in a cheaper and more convenient way to access some of the banking services that were made available 24 hours a day, seven days a week. It cost less to deploy ATM machines than to add tellers to the branch office. The customer on the other hand, does not have to rush to the bank during specific hours. It added convenience for the customers and reduced cost for the banks.

Today, we are undergoing another revolution in banking. The online banking revolution provides significantly more banking services than the ATMs. The consumer can access their savings and checking accounts or credit lines. So, the benefits to the consumer are:

- It takes less time to perform a banking transaction

- It provides banking services 24 hours a day, 7 days a week

- It simplifies record keeping

There are significant benefits to the banks from online banking.

- It costs a fraction of the expense of a teller visit to execute a computer transaction

- It allows banks to offer additional services such as stock transactions and insurance

- It enables banks to become part of online commerce by providing fund transfer abilities when a customer buys goods online

There are four types of online payment models: trusted third party systems, cash tokens, electronic checks, and credit cards. Trusted third-party systems use a holding company in which the customer has opened an account. The trusted third-party also should have the customer's credit card number or a bank account number. So when the customer makes a purchase, the holding company transfers money from the customer's bank account or credit card to the seller. Cash tokens work similar to cash. The customer obtains a cash token by paying cash. The customer can then use the token online to make purchases. The electronic check is similar to a paper check, except that it is issued online and signed by using a secret key that is known only to the user (described later in Chapter 7). A credit card number and expiration date can also be used to make online purchases.

Online banking provides convenient ways for paying bills, transferring funds, and obtaining account balance information. It can also provide more complex services such as currency exchanges, car and home mortgage loans, and establishing home equity lines. At the time of writing, there are six North Carolina banks (where I live) that offer various levels of online banking. Quoting Scarborough Research Group, Jupiter Communications, and International Data Corporation/LINK, an article in the local Raleigh N.C. newspaper (Obermayer 1996) states that the PC bank accounts in the U.S. will increase from 754,000 in 1995 to 12,980,000 by the year 2000, which is approximately an 18-fold increase.

This direction towards a digital economy also has some hurdles to cross. The online banking system must be capable of interoperating with existing banking systems. Also, the federal banking regulations may require changes to the online banking schemes. Overall, we can expect a surge in banking and commercial transactions. To allow for this, banking systems will need to have the capability to handle such an increase in the business, while providing a smooth and relatively transparent migration to the customers.

The topics of electronic commerce including the various payment models are addressed in Chapters 7 and 8.

Risks and Inhibitors to Electronic Commerce

There are two types of risks or inhibitors in attaining successful electronic commerce. The first pertains to lack of sales and the second relates to some of the legal and network security issues.

In his article (Welz 1995), Welz quotes Crain's Business Weekly about an example of a business on the Internet. It cites the story of a Russian art importer who had not sold a single painting through its presence on an Internet mall. One of the reasons for the lack of sales, as quoted in Welz's article, is the lack of understanding of the demographics of the Internet audience.

Internet Demographics

Welz (1995) provides some of the demographics of Internet users. The average household income of a family with Internet access is $66.7k, compared to the average U.S. family income of $42.4k. As stated earlier, his article quotes Forrester to predict that by the year 2000, two-thirds of the Web users will be consumers and one-third corporate and academic users. Although these demographics may change over time, the businesses must be targeted for the audience that is accessible through the Internet.

The second reason for a lack of significant online business may be that the Internet may very well not be the point of sale for a business. Instead, an Internet storefront may simply enhance the sales at the real world retail outlet. Advertising on the Internet is attractive given its low cost and easy access. It also avoids several of the security issues involved in transferring money for online sales. It may take a few years for the merchants to determine the optimal ways to sell effectively and to find and maintain repeat customers. Retailers need to demonstrate the value of electronic malls to the consumers, such as timeliness, convenience, ease of use, and potentially lower prices.

If the current indications are any guess, the trend is taking an interesting turn. Although online commerce is slow, online banking is making strong strides.

Legal Issues

"Net Liability: Getting Established on the Web is more risky than you'd think."

Kate Maddox and Clinton Wilder, *Net Liability*, Top story. Information Week.
January 8, 1996. p. 14

Although I have no intentions of addressing the various legal aspects of the Web, some interesting concerns are worth noting. Maddox and Wilder (Maddox 1996) suggest that the company's lawyers get involved before doing business in cyberspace. They feel that corporate World Wide Web sites that aren't careful may face some of the legal issues of libel, copyright infringement, and access to pornography. An executive of Gartner Group Inc., an information technology advisory firm, is quoted as stating that they have started telling their clients to get their attorneys involved to understand the legal ramifications.

Another legal concern relates to providing hot links to other home pages. In Maddox (1996), American Airlines parent AMR Corporation is mentioned as an example. AMR is quite concerned about providing hot links to other hotels and resorts from their home page. There are many hotels and resorts who would like to have a hot link from the AMR home page, and although most are legitimate, AMR cannot be responsible for policing everyone. They are guarding against the possibility, for example, that a traveller gets fraudulently billed from a Web site linked to AMR's home page and tries to hold AMR responsible.

Finally, we want to identify a well-known legal concern relating to secure commerce. On the Internet, there is no face-to-face human interaction. As such, consumers do not show a driver's licence to identify themselves, do not sign credit card receipts in the presence of a sales clerk, and are not assured that no unauthorized person is copying their credit card information. So, for online commerce, we need an electronic equivalent of a driver's licence. As stated earlier, we also need to provide the legally acceptable proof that the consumer indeed (electronically) signed the purchase order and received the goods. Finally, someone has to assume the liability in case the credit card number is stolen over the Internet. The security aspects of this topic were mentioned earlier under *Secure Commerce*.

Technology Trends

The Internet is attracting the best innovations in the areas of computer usability and network exploitation. Internet browsers and servers continue to rush forward to include access to existing information resources as well as innovative ways to access the Internet.

The first wave of innovations included provisions for local Internet system services such as directory and security. New protocols were developed to provide security for Web browsers and servers. This wave also included basic tools to access documents on the Web, facilities to publish documents, and to link Web documents. The next wave included new search tools on the Web, enhanced publishing tools as well as streaming video. New technologies are being introduced by the day. By the time this book is published, several of my comments will move from the future to the present, and from the present to the past.

Some of the interesting Internet technologies include:

- Interactive Yellow Pages
- Virtual Post Office
- Electronic Harassment
- Politics on the Internet
- Virtual Reality
- New Publishing Approaches
- Real-Time News
- Broadcast Video
- 3-Dimensional Images
- 3-Dimensional effects such as a walk through the museums or a stroll through Tivoli gardens

There are some difficult social issues facing the growth of Internet. Ethics on the Internet and the issue of pornography must be addressed quickly.

This trend of innovations will continue. The immediate frontier is the broad-scale offering and use of electronic commerce. A continuum of new security technologies will make them pervasive for most transactions on the Internet (there are few messages encrypted on the Internet at this time). New programming techniques to bring in remote software for execution on a Web will continue, such as with Java.

There also will be customized packages for us on the Internet. It is conceivable that the banking community may distribute their own home terminal with preloaded software for transacting banking business from home.

We are in the midst of a major information revolution!

The overall topic of online commerce has been addressed by various authors. Besides some of the papers referenced in this chapter, there are other books (Loshin 1995, Mathiesen 1995) that address the marketing and related topics for online commerce.

Security Breaches

"...You don't need a gun to steal."

Beth Morris, "Crime Fighters Open Chapter in Rock Hill,"
Carolina Computer News. April 1996. p. 1.

Network security has often been recognized as an inhibitor to the growth of business on the Internet. According to the Third Annual Ernst & Young/Information Week Information Security Survey, 87% of those currently using the Internet, 66% of those not using the Internet currently, and 83% of those planning to use the Internet within a year stated that they would increase the use of the Internet for business purposes if security was enhanced. In the next four chapters we discuss the underlying elements of network and Internet security that are pivotal to obtaining secure commerce on the Internet.

In many instances, the Internet is becoming the medium for unauthorized access to private networks. By exploiting the connectivity of thousands of private businesses to the Internet, a hacker can find unauthorized ways to access a private network. Additionally, the attacker can intercept, decipher, and interpret or even modify the data as it traverses the Internet. In some cases, the attackers have hijacked sessions by using some of the well-known spoofing attacks discussed later in this chapter.

The topic of Internet security breaches is diverse and complex. To begin, the intruder may be driven by one of several motives to breach a private network. These motives range from financial gains to industrial espionage. Once they have gained access, an attacker can inflict a variety of damages and steal information, resources, or money. There are several symptoms and approaches that can detect when a breach is underway. If it appears that your network is under attack, there are certain measures to minimize the impact. Finally, there are tools and strategies to test your software and minimize the exposures to security breaches. In the following, we address each of these topics.

Motives

Three types of motives are commonly behind network security breaches: industrial espionage, financial gains, and revenge or publicity.

Industrial Espionage

Industrial espionage pertains to the theft of industry secrets for competitive advantages. An attacker penetrates a company's private files, searches for company secrets, and sells them to a competitor. An important goal of the attacker is to prevent the attacked site from determining that its security has been compromised.

Industrial espionage is a growing concern as increasing numbers of private businesses attach to the Internet. According to Winkler (1996), the Federal Bureau of Investigation estimates that U.S. corporations lose $100 billion annually due to industrial espionage.

Recent studies have shown that businesses are often exposed to significant internal risks from disgruntled or dishonest employees. Winkler (1996) outlines a case study in which a penetration test was conducted for a large corporation. The objective was to simulate an industrial espionage attack against the company within the constraints of the funding. The attack included collecting the publicly available information, obtaining a temporary position in the company, misusing and misrepresenting the position, abusing physical access, internal hacking, and using external hackers. According to the paper, within one day, over $1,000,000,000 of information was stolen.

Winkler also quotes a study by Michigan State University indicating that insiders were the source of greater losses by a factor of 20 to 1. According to a brochure by Trident Data Systems (Trident 1996), 8 out of 10 network break-ins are inside jobs.

Another aspect of industrial espionage relates to attacking government networks for sensitive information. According to Anthes (1995), the Pentagon's Center for Information Systems Security (CISS) attempts to penetrate defense networks. It states that hackers are able to gain unauthorized access 95% of time; only 5% of them are detected, and of those, less than 5% are reported to senior officers.

Financial Gains

Financial gain is another common goal for network breaches.
The attacker gains unauthorized access and then steals money
or resources to make money. A dishonest employee transfers
the money from the company's account to his or her private
account. A disgruntled laid-off employee may seek revenge by
stealing money before leaving the company. A hacker on the
Internet may gain unauthorized access to a bank's system and
transfer funds.

Revenge or Publicity

Networks may also be breached to seek revenge or to gain publicity. A fired employee may seek revenge by leaving behind a
time bomb or Trojan horse (described later in this chapter) to
damage the company's network. Sometimes, hackers seek publicity by demonstrating their skills to break into networks.
Some vendors have offered rewards for successful break-ins to
their network security products.

Threats

A threat is defined as the potential to exploit a weakness that
may result in an unauthorized access, disclosure of information
or consumption, theft or destruction of a resource. Some types
of threats are:

- Administrator Errors
- Wiretaps
- Viruses
- Hackers
- Competitors
- Dishonest or disgruntled employees

Types of Attacks

Internet security breaches can be divided into the following types of attacks.

Denial of Service

A *denial of service* attack prevents some resources of the network from functioning according to their intended purposes. Denial of service attacks include actions that lead to unauthorized destruction, modification, or delay of service. It may range from a lack of available memory or disk space to a partial shutdown of the network. Typically, a denial of service attack leaves one or more hosts incapable of servicing their users. In some attacks, the overall network performance is severely impacted, which in turn leads to denial of service for the network users. Details on denial of service attack can be found in Needham (1994).

Fraud

In a *fraud,* the attacker uses unauthorized means to steal or to transfer money to another account. Sometimes, such an attack is launched by compromising user passwords.

Breach of Confidentiality

Confidentiality protects information from unauthorized disclosure. A *breach of confidentiality* implies that secret data has been disclosed to unauthorized parties. This breach is often accomplished by stealing or guessing the cryptographic key used for data encryption and decryption. A common approach to guessing the keys is to launch a brute-force attack. Such an attack attempts every possible hexadecimal combination until the correct encryption key is determined, as described below.

Resource Theft

Resource theft occurs when unauthorized individuals gain access to a resource and transfer the information to other parties. This sort of an attack may result from a breach of confidentiality or from a theft of user passwords. Most industrial espionage activities are aimed at stealing resources through unauthorized means.

Brute-Force Attacks

A *brute-force attack* involves the use of a computer to attempt all possible keys. Consider an encryption algorithm such as the *Data Encryption Standard (DES)* described in Chapter 2. DES uses 56-bit keys for data encryption and decryption, so the attacker writes a program to attempt every possible 56-bit key. The program executes each binary value of 56-bit keys until the resultant output equals the original plaintext. In this case, the attacking program will attempt at most 2^{56} keys.

A brute-force attack is always possible. However, you can take certain steps to reduce the potential of a successful brute-force attack. The brute-force attack can be made extremely expensive in terms of money and time, such that only a few intruders would consider launching this attack. However, with advances in computing, it is getting cheaper and faster to launch such attacks. Schneier (1995) treats this subject in great detail. He also provides estimates for the amount of time it would take to launch successful brute-force attacks against various schemes and algorithms.

Cryptanalysis

Cryptanalysis is the science of breaking the ciphertext. It is also called the science that obtains the plaintext message from an encrypted message without the use of key, as shown in Figure 2.9. A *cryptanalyst* is a person who practices cryptanalysis. There are five types of cryptanalytic attack. Here, we describe them in the order of their potential to be successful.

1. *Ciphertext-only attack*: In this attack, the cryptana-lyst has several encrypted messages available. The

goal of the attack is to deduce the plaintext of as many messages as possible. In addition, the cryptanalyst has to determine the cryptographic key (or keys) to decrypt other messages that are encrypted using the same keys.

2. *Known-plaintext attack*: The cryptanalyst has access to several encrypted messages as well as to the corresponding plaintext messages. The cryptanalyst's job is to determine the key (or keys) in order to decrypt other messages encrypted with the same key (or keys).

3. *Chosen-plaintext attack*: In this attack, the cryptanalyst can obtain encrypted text for a chosen plaintext message. In addition, the cryptanalyst has access to other plaintext and to corresponding encrypted messages. This attack is more powerful than the preceding attack since the cryptanalyst can create plaintext of his or her choice which can yield more information in determining the key.

4. *Adaptive-chosen-plaintext attack*: This attack is more powerful than the chosen-plaintext attack. Here the cryptanalyst can repeatedly obtain encrypted text by changing the plaintext based on the results of the previous encryption.

5. *Chosen-ciphertext attack*: In this attack, the cryptanalyst can specify different ciphertexts to be decrypted and has access to the corresponding plaintext.

Kocher (1995) describes the use of timing attacks in cryptanalysis of Diffie-Hellman, RSA, DSS, and other systems. This approach is based on using the time taken to perform cryptographic operations. Other references on cryptanalysis include Schneier (1994) and Simmons (1994); Schneier (1994) provides a good introduction to this topic.

Major Break-Ins

Given its open access for users and wide-spread connectivity to almost everywhere, the Internet is a favorite target for most hackers and intruders. The number of security breaches is increasing rapidly. According to the Computer Emergency Response Team at Carnegie Mellon University (CERTB 1995), they receive an average of three new computer security incidents every day. Many Internet breaches are publicized and attract the attention of the network community, while numerous incidents go unnoticed. In the following, we describe some of the significant breaches that have taken place in the last few years. As depicted in Table 1.1, it can be seen that the number of major Internet attacks has been on the increase over the last few years.

Year	Title	Description
1988	Internet Worm	Impacted a large number of Internet hosts
1989	Hacker in Cuckoo's Egg	East German spy penetrates U.S. Defense network; Caught by Cliff Stoll by accident
1993	N.Y. City Break-in	Intruder intercepted logon traffic and stole IDs and passwords
1995	Source Address Spoofing	Denial of Service using source address spoofing
1995	Bank Fraud	$10M stolen from Citibank; most of the stolen money was recovered
1996	Penetration into U.S. Government Network	Detected by U.S. Government using wire-tap on Internet
1996	Word Macro Virus	Multiple Viruses that inflict Denial of Service

Table 1.1: Major Internet Breaches

1988: Internet Worm

On November 2, 1988, the Internet suffered one of its worst attacks. The attack, called *Internet Worm,* was a self-replicating program that spread across the Internet in a few hours. Some estimates state that as many an 7000 hosts were impacted. Many hosts were shutdown and several others experienced severe performance degradation.

This worm was created by Robert T. Morris. He exploited the weaknesses in three TCP/IP applications: *FINGERD, RHOST,* and *SENDMAIL.* At his trial in January 1990, Mr. Morris argued that his objective was to demonstrate weaknesses in the Internet and was not with any malice. He was convicted under the Computer Fraud and Abuse Act (1986) and was given three years probation, a $10,000 fine, and 400 hours of community service.

The Internet Worm gained publicity and lead to increased awareness of security issues on the Internet. The Computer Emergency Response Team (CERT) at Carnegie Mellon University was created after this attack. Additional information on this attack can be found in Clark (1991, 64).

1989: Hacker in "Cuckoo's Egg"

Cliff Stoll, an astronomer, was working as a system administrator and tracking an accounting error of 75 cents. In the process, he detected that an intruder from East Germany was attempting to gain access to U.S. government computers in Europe. Stoll tracked the intruder for some time. During a period of 10 months, the intruder attacked approximately 450 computers and successfully gained access to 35 of them. It is estimated that the intruder was attempting to penetrate the system for as long as one year prior to detection.

The attacker seemed to be an expert, using multiple entry points to hide the attack. In one instance, the intruder implanted a trapdoor (described later in this chapter) that was used a year later. The attacker seemed to be interested in sensitive information such as user passwords.

Stoll describes this attack in his book, *The Cuckoo's Egg* (Stoll 1990). His disclosure resulted in an investigation that included many governments and agencies.

This break-in is also described in Clark (1991, 62).

1993: N.Y. City Internet Break-In

In October 1993, an Internet public access system reported that someone had been stealing userIDs and passwords, thereby compromising the security of several sites. The intruder was recording the IDs and passwords by exploiting weaknesses in the *SENDMAIL* program. This attack exploited a different weakness in the SENDMAIL program than that utilized by the Internet worm. The intrusion was detected when the system administrator stumbled into one of the intruder's files. This attack was described in OST (1993, 19).

In the last few years, enhanced versions of SENDMAIL have been developed to address its various well-known vulnerabilities.

1995: Source Address Spoofing Attack

The Source Address Spoofing attack was reported in a warning by CERT on January 23, 1995. This attack exploited the weakness that a TCP/IP host does not necessarily validate the source address of the packet. As a result, an attacking host can send packets on behalf of another host. Such attacks impact the applications that use IP addresses for authenticating users. This particular attack also bypassed the intervening firewall.

At least 50 hosts were affected including the San Diego Center for Supercomputing and Stanford Linear Accelerator Computing Center.

There are certain precautions to address such attacks. Clearly, it is difficult to require each host to change their software so that the source address is validated. However, the firewall configuration can be adapted to resist some attacks of this sort. This is because, in most cases, the attacker is going to impersonate someone, such as the network administrator, from inside the private network. Note that the network resources are often controlled by employees or administrators from within the company. So the attacking host will be from the Internet, but it will send packets on behalf of a host that is inside the private network. To resist such an attack, the firewall can be configured so that if a packet arrives from the Internet with a source address of a host inside the private network, then the firewall should discard that packet, as we will describe in Chapter 4.

Additional details on this attack can be found in Ahuja (1996), and Jolitz (1995).

1995: Bank Fraud

On August 17, 1995, Vladimir Levin was charged by U.S. prosecutors for tapping into Citibank more than 40 times and transferring at least $10 million to other bank accounts. U.S. prosecutors asked a London court to extradite Levin. In this case, the target was Citibank's fund transfer system in Manhattan. Four other suspected accomplices were also arrested. All but $400,000 was recovered. This attack was reported in Caldwell (1995).

1996: U.S. Military Computers Penetration

"This is a case of cybersleuthing, a glimpse of what computer crime-fighting will look like in the coming years."

Donald Stern, U.S. Attorney in Boston. *News and Observer*.
Raleigh, NC March 30, 1996. p. 5A.

On March 30, 1996, U.S. newspapers reported that through a wiretap on the Internet, federal agents had tracked down an intruder. They charged Julio Cesar Ardita, a 22-year old computer science student in Argentina, with conducting illegal computer entries from Argentina.

According to the news report, Ardita first broke into the computer of Harvard University's Faculty of Arts and Sciences. The break-ins occurred between July 12 and December 28, 1995. Ardita stole passwords of some of the 16,500 legitimate users and used the Harvard computer as the platform to penetrate into U.S. military computers on the Internet. He gained access to sensitive and confidential government information, but not classified national security files, according to Stern. During November/December 1995, a court-ordered wiretap was placed in the Harvard computer. This was the first time a court-ordered wiretap had been used to track a person making criminal use of a computer, according to U.S. Attorney General Janet Reno, quoted in U.S. newspapers.

1996: Word Macro Viruses

The *Word Macro* viruses spread by means of auto-executing macros written in Microsoft WordBasic on all versions of Windows as well as the MAC. The *concept virus (winword.concept)* affects print and save functions on large Word documents. Other Word Macro viruses include *hot virus*, which deletes word documents when they are opened; *colors virus*, which changes color settings to randomly selected colors on Windows; *Format C virus*, which deletes files on hard drives; and *atom virus*, which deletes files in the current directory on December 13. These viruses infect Microsoft Word 2.0 or higher documents operating on Windows 3.1, Windows 95, Windows NT, and the MAC operating system. Antivirus companies are introducing products to disinfect the Word Macro viruses. This information on Word virus was obtained from Cobb (1996) and Violino (1996). Cobb (1996) narrates his personal experience with the concept virus; he received the virus while using the Internet.

National Computer Security Association (NCSA) conducted a survey that is quoted in Violino (1996). Of the 300 large North American companies surveyed, 50% stated that they were hit by the macro virus attacks in January/February 1996. Of those hit, 12% stated that they had 25 or more PCs that were impacted at the same site and at the same time.

Other Break-Ins

A brief review of some of the other attacks follows. The following information is based on Russell (1991).

Bank Theft

A branch manager manipulates a computer system to avoid the audit checking and transfers $25 million. This attack occurred in 1984.

Friday the 13th Virus

In January 1988, it was discovered that thousands of students at Hebrew University in Jerusalem were infected by the *Friday the 13th virus*. This virus was scheduled to erase the hard disks of financial, research, and administrative computers on May 13th, 1988. This virus appeared again at the Royal National Institute for the Blind in England and erased months of work. It also appeared in the United States as the Columbus Day virus.

White House Computers

While working for the Tower Commission on the Iran-Contra affair, a researcher explored the computers used by Oliver North. He discovered that some of the sensitive notes had been deleted from the White House computers and were dumped into a mainframe. As a result, this information was available to the users of the mainframe computers. This incident took place in 1988 and raised concerns about the security of White House computer systems.

Airline System

A major travel agency discovered that its reservation and ticketing system had been penetrated. As a result, someone could illegally print airline tickets. This incident occurred in 1988 and raised alarm since a terrorist organization could penetrate the reservation system and obtain passenger information to plan attacks.

Satellite Positioning System

In 1989, a Kansas student penetrates the Air Force Satellite positioning system. This 14-year-old student used an Apple home computer to dial illegal long-distance access codes to break into the Air Force system. The student also gained access and browsed through confidential files of more than 200 businesses.

NASA Computer

In 1990, a NASA computer in Norfolk, Virginia was shut down for 24 hours. An Australian student, who called himself *Phoenix*, was charged. Apparently, the student penetrated into several Australian and U.S. computers and also made "alterations to data" on a computer at Lawrence Livermore Laboratory in California.

There are several other breaches that are not presented here; for other examples, see Baran (1990).

Viruses

Viruses have been affecting computer users for several years. According to an NCSA (National Computer Security Association) survey quoted in Violino (1996), it is estimated that losses to U.S. companies from all computer viruses in 1996 will be $5 billion to $6 billion, compared to $1 billion for 1995.

A *virus* is a self-reproducing program that can infect and damage other programs. When a virus is executed, it makes one or more copies of itself. When those copies are executed, they make more copies, ad infinitum. Besides viruses, there are certain other forms of malicious programs that can also inflict damage, as shown in Table 1.2

	Can Replicate Itself	Host Program Required
Viruses	Yes	Yes
Bacteria	Yes	No
Worms	Yes	No
Trapdoors	No	Yes
Logic Bombs	No	Yes
Trojan Horses	No	Yes

Table 1.2: Classes of Malicious Programs

Bacteria are programs that duplicate themselves and grow exponentially. Although a bacteria does not attack another program, it can inflict denial of service by simply replicating itself and its copies, thereby consuming the system memory or disk space.

Worms are programs that replicate themselves and spread to different sites on a network. A worm does not attack other programs but can consume network resources. The famous Internet Worm, described earlier, brought down a large part of the Internet network in 1988.

A *trapdoor* provides an undocumented entry to a program. Trapdoors bypass normal system protection and are used by programmers to trace, monitor, debug, or even apply fixes to a program. A trapdoor provides easy access to large programs and may be misused if disclosed to unauthorized persons. One such story is presented in the 1983 movie *WarGames*.

A *logic bomb* is a piece of code that is programmed to inflict damage when certain conditions are met. A logic bomb is not a standalone program; as such it must reside within another program to locate itself. A logic bomb is also called a *time bomb*. A common example of a logic bomb is when a particular program is set to execute at a certain time in the future. A logic bomb commonly is used when vendors distribute sample software free of charge for a limited time. In this way, a customer can use the software for some time to gain experience, but cannot use it beyond the specified time without making the payment and resetting the logic bomb or purchasing the software.

A *Trojan horse* is a piece of code that is implanted inside another program to perform a disguised function. As such, a Trojan horse hides inside another program and does not exist independently. Thompson (1984) modified the C compiler using the concept of a Trojan horse.

The term Trojan horse comes from Greek mythology. A Trojan horse was a large hollow horse made of wood in which the Greeks hid their soldiers. The Greeks left the Trojan horse at the gates of Troy, and the Trojans took the horse inside. Later, the soldiers came out of the wooden horse and opened the gates for Greeks, which led the Greeks to win the war.

Viruses are described in detail in the book by Ludwig (1990). Phillips (1995a, 1995b) provides an overview and comparison on antivirus products. Kohlhepp (1996) provides a review of a virus-scanning software. The topic of protecting Windows 95 from viruses is discussed in Sullivan (1995).

Breach Detection

A major network security breach usually can be detected by monitoring the general network behavior. Typically, some of the hosts may be shut down or demonstrate unusually poor performance. However, it is quite difficult to detect breaches that affect only a few hosts or cause an unnoticeable performance degradation or denial of service. It is also quite difficult to detect breaches that are designed to prevent detection. Although such breaches may lead to a significant loss, their existence is not apparently obvious to a casual system administrator.

A simple approach to detect a security breach is to monitor any significant change in the system behavior. Once your system detects an unusual change, you should investigate whether the network is under attack. Some of the common observations are:

- Sudden change in the number of transactions received or transmitted from your Web site

- Sudden increase in the response time to selected commands or inquiries

- Sudden depletion of memory or available space on hard drive

- Persistent logon attempts from any one workstation using different IDs

- Persistent logon attempts from several workstations using the same ID or group of IDs

- Receipt of unusually large files that are depleting your hard drive

- Alarms indicating unauthorized access to secret files, for example, the password database

There are several approaches to implement a breach-detection scheme. These schemes can be implemented in the firewall or the audit trail system. In addition, it helps to educate the user community on this topic and solicit their feedback on any unusual network behavior.

When implemented in the firewall, the system administrator can observe the behavior of unsuccessful logon attempts, check for viruses, or monitor the size of files transferring across the firewall. Such an implementation can operate in real time where detection of an exceptional behavior can alert the system administrator.

In addition, software can be implemented to constantly monitor the audit records. For example, if someone is logging from different workstations using the same userID and different passwords, then such behavior may be cause for alarm. The software continuously can observe the cumulative behavior for the last several hours and can report any suspicious trends. An intrusion detection model is described in Denning (1987).

Finally, the network administrator can ask the users to watch for any unusual behavior. In addition, the system administrator can also distribute a list of potential symptoms that should be reported.

Breach Recovery

Once it is determined that the network is under attack, the system administrator may take certain actions to minimize the impact, as follows.

1. Disconnect any access to your network from outside the network, including the Internet. For example, when the Source Address Spoofing attack was discovered at the Stanford Linear Accelerator (SLAC), the administrators cut off all external network access to the facility.

   In certain cases, it may be preferable to disconnect all the internal connections from the firewall, until the breach is fixed.

2. Assess the damage to each resource and create a plan for recovery.

3. Use the backup system to reload the previous level of your system software. It is critical that the system is backed up at frequent intervals.

4. Initiate an inquiry into the causes of the break-in and list the near-term and long-term plans to resist similar attacks in the future.

At SLAC, the network was only partially recovered in two days. Approaches to test a network for potential security weaknesses are described later.

Breach Avoidance

To avoid network breaches, there are two complementary approaches. First, the security industry has developed software test tools that can be used to identify potential vulnerabilities. These tools detect network weaknesses by attempting to penetrate a given network or a software product. Secondly, the network administrator must develop a strategy that minimizes risks and breaches.

Tools

The Internet security industry is growing rapidly to embrace the issues of testing networks for security holes. As of this writing, several tools are available in the marketplace. PC Week (Surkan 1996) analyzes four such tools:

- *Pingware* from Bellcore
- *Internet Scanner* from Internet Security Systems, Inc.
- *NetProbe* from Qualix Group, Inc.
- *SATAN* distributed as freeware by Dan Farmer and Wietse Venema

According to ISS (1996), the Internet Scanner runs on UNIX systems and probes each device on the network for potential vulnerabilities. It checks for over 120 potential security vulnerabilities. The devices may be running on a UNIX host, Microsoft NT/Windows 95 system, firewall, router, Web server, or PC. Details on the Internet Scanner can be found in ISS (1996) and Surkan (1996).

Security Administrator's Tool for Analyzing Networks (SATAN) is available as freeware by accessing *http://www.fish.com*. SATAN helps system administrators identify several common networking-related security problems. SATAN remotely tests the networks and collects information on the security holes. It also provides a description of the vulnerability and suggests approaches to address them. SATAN provides a flexible approach for testing by aiming the test on a single host, multiple hosts on a network, or hosts connected to the target host. The testing can expand to target various levels of hosts attached to the target host system. By adding PERL scripts, SATAN's testing can be expanded. Details on SATAN can be found by accessing *http://www.fish.com*. Other references on SATAN include CERT (1995).

Services

To help a company determine its vulnerabilities, some vendors offer ethical penetration services. These services include testing your network for any vulnerabilities and reporting the results. Winkler (1996) describes a similar approach to analyze a company's weaknesses described earlier under Industrial Espionage.

Strategies

Strategies for avoiding security breaches consist of implementing various approaches embodied in sound security policies. Once a security policy has been established, the company can implement approaches using state-of-the-art security technologies. Some of the technologies that are relevant to online com-

merce are outlined in this chapter. Other security books present
the network issues and approaches to address those issues,
including Ahuja (1996), Amoroso (1994), Clark (1991), Shaffer
(1994), and Russell (1991).

To minimize risks, you can implement several schemes and
technologies to achieve the desired goals. The remainder of this
book provides descriptions of approaches to achieve Internet
security and secure commerce.

Every secure network must implement appropriate authentication and encryption schemes to provide secure communications among its users. The workstations and servers on the
network must use secure operating systems. This topic is
described in detail in the next chapter.

To use the Internet, the private network must ensure that
appropriate security schemes are implemented for applications
that communicate over the Internet. The topic of securing
Internet applications is described in detail in Chapter 3.

In addition, the private network must protect itself from unauthorized intrusions and attacks from the Internet. To address
this requirement, most private networks are implementing firewalls. The topic of firewalls is presented in Chapter 4.

The related topic of securely transacting commerce on the
Internet is addressed in Chapters 5, 6, 7, and 8.

In effect, the whole purpose of network security technologies is
to protect resources, authenticate the sources, securely transport private or secret information, and transact secure commerce on the Internet.

Security Concepts

"Security: ... Freedom from danger,
Something that secures,
Measures taken to guard against espionage or
sabotage, crime, attack or escape,.."

Webster's New Collegiate Dictionary. Henry Bosley Woolf,
Editor-in-Chief G. & C. Merriam Company. 1977. p. 1045

Corporations require secure and reliable networks to transact business. Businesses must protect their confidential data against eavesdropping and thefts. Banks require a foolproof method to verify user identity before permitting major funds transfer. Users must feel free to exchange secret information without concerns for interception or loss of data.

To address these requirements, network security relies on the concept of protecting the critical assets while allowing open and convenient exchange of information.

It has been argued that the goal of open networking conflicts with network security. In my view, this statement is true only in its extremities. A totally secure network is one that has *no* connections to the outside world. On the other hand, a completely open network must permit unrestricted access from the external world. It is the goal of network security schemes to provide an open environment that is also secure. Given all the risks and threats that surround private networks, several technologies are emerging to protect resources as well as support secure communications.

Security over the Internet entails a variety of requirements and approaches. A key objective is for a workstation on a private network to be capable of securely and reliably communicating with another entity on the private network or the Internet. Additionally, we would like users to be able to store or access resources securely within the private network or across the Internet, as shown in Figure 2.1.

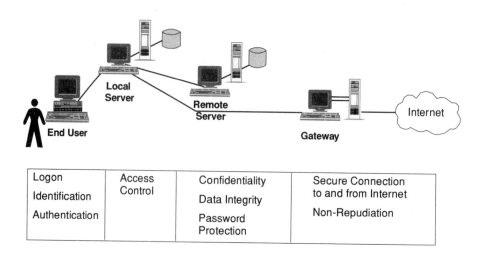

Logon Identification Authentication	Access Control	Confidentiality Data Integrity Password Protection	Secure Connection to and from Internet Non-Repudiation

Figure 2.1: End - End Security

Let us consider the requirements to provide security for the network shown in Figure 2.1. These requirements range from identifying and verifying the user or a program to assuring the integrity and secrecy of data during transmission. Table 2.1 outlines the requirements along with the corresponding concepts and technologies.

Requirement	Concept	Technologies
Identify user	Identification	UserIDs
Verify user identity	Authentication	Passwords or credentials
Restrict resource access	Access control	Access control lists (ACLs)
Provide different levels of resource access	Authorization	Access rights in ACLs
Protect data privacy	Confidentiality	Encryption
Detect data tampering during transmission	Data integrity	Message digest
Callable security services from applications	Security API[*]	GSSAPI,[**] GCSAPI,[***] GASAPI[****]
Verify message origin	Source authentication	Digital signature (Chapter 5)
Establish proof that the sender sent the data and receiver received it	Nonrepudiation	X.509 Certificates (Chapter 5)

* API: Application Program Interface
** GSSAPI: Generic Security Service API
***GCSAPI: Generic Cryptographic Service API
****GASAPI: Generic Audit Service API

Table 2.1: Security Concepts

To begin, users must identify themselves to an application program or a security system. A security system may be located at the client workstation or a security server. The security system (or the application) must verify the claimed identity of the user. In addition, the security system should enforce appropriate levels of access to the resources. This is accomplished by assigning access rights and enforcing them through access control. Next, we must protect the secrecy of any private data by encrypting it. However, encrypted data may also be tampered by an intruder during transmission. To protect the integrity of data, we can use the message digest technology described later. By encrypting the message digest, we can also authenticate the origin of the message, as we will describe in Chapter 5.

Finally, in a client/server network, applications require access to security services to encrypt the data or to ensure data integrity during transmission. These services should be available to applications through API calls.

Before proceeding to describe the preceding concepts, we must address the topic of nonrepudiation. Nonrepudiation establishes the proof that the sender indeed sent the data or that the receiver really received it. It protects the receiver from the sender falsely denying that the data was sent. It also protects the sender from the receiver falsely denying that the data was received.

This requirement can be best illustrated through an example. An investor decides to sell a large number of shares, so she sends the request to her stock broker and the stock broker sells the stocks. Now the stock price rises sharply, and the investor denies that she sent the order to sell the stocks. Conversely, it is possible that under reverse circumstances, the stock broker may deny receiving the order to sell the stock. In this type of situation, it is easy to see that nonrepudiation support is critical for transacting commerce over the Internet. This topic is addressed in detail in Chapter 5.

Identification

A user can be uniquely identified by an identifier assigned to the user. A user identifier is also called a *userid*, *userID*, or simply *ID*. Often, the security system assigns a unique ID to each user. However, sometimes users can select their own ID as long as it has not already been assigned to another user. For example, my ID for e-mail is

vahuja @ vnet.ibm.com

It is desirable for a user to have the same ID throughout the network. Although there may be several applications that the user may wish to log on, he or she preferably should have the same ID. A single ID for each user across the network implies that the user does not have to remember several IDs. As a result, there is less of a chance that the user will forget the ID, commit mistakes, and require access to the system administrator. A common ID for the user is also beneficial to the security system because it avoids the overhead needed to maintain records for multiple IDs.

Authentication

Authentication is the process of verifying the identity of a user. Authentication is accomplished by sharing a secret between the user and the server. By far, the most commonly used secret between the user and the server is the *password*. After entering the ID, the server prompts the user to enter the password as shown in Figure 2.2. The user enters the password, the server compares it with the password stored for that ID in its data-base, and the user is authenticated if there is a match.

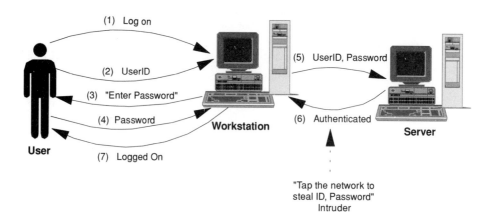

Figure 2.2: Log On Process

Passwords have two types of security exposures: they can be guessed or stolen.

Password Guessing

Password guessing is the process of correctly guessing the pass-word of a legitimate user. Users select passwords that are easy to remember. Consequently, such passwords can be easily guessed. Klein (1990) has analyzed the password guessing attacks for approximately 15,000 user accounts. He began by collecting a variety of information about the users. He also included some general words such as names of movies, movie stars, players, games, and so on. He used four DECstation

3100s, each capable of checking approximately 750 passwords per second. As a result, he could guess approximately 2.7% of the passwords in the first 15 minutes and 21% (approximately 3000 passwords) within the first week.

Passwords can also be guessed by applying a brute-force attack. In such an attack, the attacker attempts every possible combination of the alphabet to construct a word of the same size as the attacked password. Clearly, such an attack requires significant computational power. However, for any password guessing approach the attacker cannot repeatedly attempt to use the logon process for launching the attack because most security systems will lock out a userid after two or three unsuccessful log on attempts. As a result, many attacks to steal passwords are targeted at gaining access to the password database. Even though such data may be stored in some encrypted form, the attacker can launch a brute-force attack to recover the plaintext passwords. At the same time, to protect passwords during transmission, many systems accept the userid and the encrypted password, as described next.

Password Theft

Passwords can be stolen while in transmission. As shown in Figure 2.2, a password can be intercepted and interpreted by an intruder. There are two approaches to resist such an attack. The passwords can be encrypted for transmission over the network, as mentioned earlier, or the network can implement a one-time password scheme, described later.

A password can be protected by encrypting it at the sender workstation and decrypting it at the receiver workstation. However, such protection has a limited value. Consider the example when an intruder intercepts and steals an encrypted password. Assume that the same encryption scheme is in place for some length of time. So, at a later time, the intruder can replay the userID and the encrypted password to gain access to the system, as shown in Figure 2.3. This will succeed only if the real user is not already logged on and if the encryption scheme (key) has not changed. It is important to note that this attack succeeds even if the encryption scheme is sufficiently strong and the intruder cannot recover the plaintext password. The reason is that the receiving system will accept an encrypted password. This is called *password replay* attack. We will discuss the topic of encryption later in this chapter.

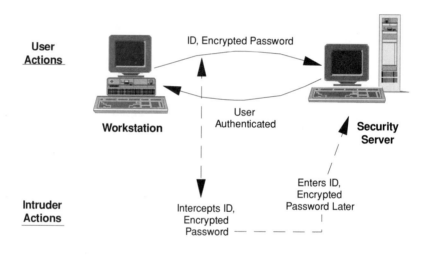

Figure 2.3: Replay Attack Using Encrypted Passwords

One-Time Passwords

The concept of the *one-time password* is to dynamically generate unpredictable passwords that are valid for a single access to the security system. A second attempt to log on using the same one-time password will generate an error and result in rejection of the logon request. The one-time passwords often are implemented using token cards, although some software-based implementations also exist. Since the one-time passwords cannot be reused, their theft should not pose the security risks described earlier.

With a *token card*, the user enters a PIN code through a keypad on the card. A PIN code is a secret number that the user must save or remember. As such, the PIN code reduces the risk if the token card is lost. The card has a built-in processor that verifies the PIN code and generates a random number. The user enters that number as the one-time password for the logon process. The security server verifies the password as follows. At the set-up time, an application is installed in the security server that can also generate the same number for a given userID. Upon receipt of the one-time password from the user, the security server forwards the userID to this application to generate the corresponding random number. The two numbers are compared and if there is a match, the user is authenticated. This scheme is shown in Figure 2.4. If an intruder steals the one-time password, it cannot be reused again. Since the number is generated based on time, it is invalid after a very short time. If the same one-time password is sent within the short time window, then the security system can remember the previous use of the password and reject the second use. Vendors have developed and marketed schemes that are based on variations of this basic approach.

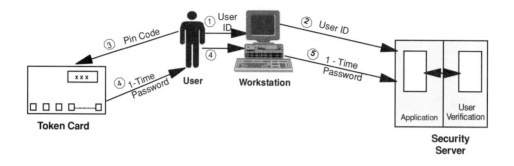

Figure 2.4: Token Card Authentication

The topic of password security has been addressed by several authors and continues to be a topic of strong interest. Other references on this topic include Ahuja (1996), Bishop (1992), Bishop (1990), De Alvaré (1990), Johnson (1995), Raleigh (1988), Morris (1979), Edwards (1993), and Spafford (1992).

Third-Party Authentication

Before initiating any communication in a client/server network, the communicating parties may require mutual authentication. To begin, consider the simple case when a client authenticates itself to a server. In this case, it is assumed that the server has the valid identity and there is no need to authenticate it to the client. This is called *one-way authentication*, as shown in Figure 2.5a.

Next, a *two-way authentication* requires that both the client and the server authenticate themselves to each other. To accomplish that, the two-way authentication scheme assigns a password each to the client and the server. This is shown in Figure 2.5b. However, as the network size grows, the maintenance and updates of the passwords can quickly become cumbersome and time-consuming. For example, a small network of 20 clients and 5 servers will require maintenance and updates of 25 passwords in each client and server machine. The problem of coordinating and updating several passwords across the network can be addressed through the use of a trusted third party.

A *trusted third party* provides authentication for several clients and servers. The user passwords are stored in the trusted third-party machine. For a client or a server to initiate communication, they must exchange secrets with the trusted third party. In simple terms, the trusted third party authenticates the client to the server and the server to the client. Once authenticated, the client and server can initiate data exchange. The basic concept behind a third-party authentication is shown in Figure 2.5c.

The most commonly used trusted third-party scheme is called *Kerberos*. Kerberos provides two-way authentication and distribution of encryption keys. Kerberos was developed at Massachusetts Institute of Technology (MIT) and is based on a scheme developed by Needham (1978) and Schroeder.

The actual third-party authentication protocols are quite complex. Details on the Kerberos system can be found in Ahuja (1996), Stallings (1995), Stallings (1994), Lunt (1990), and Steiner (1988).

A *single logon* provides the capability for a user to [access sev]eral network resources by logging on once to the sec[urity sys]tem. Typically, a user logs on four to six times a day. [For each] system, the user may have to log on and enter an ID [and a] password. For example, I may need one ID and passw[ord to] access a database server, another ID and password to lo[g on a] TELNET server, another ID and password to log on a [Web] server, and so on. For such an environment, the user ha[s to] remember and enter several IDs and passwords. So, it can [only] be expected that the user sometimes will forget the passwo[rd] or enter a wrong password. I have heard some estimates th[at] each user typically forgets at least one password in a month. Such errors lead to a loss of productivity for the user and additional work for the system administrator. Single logon addresses these problems by requiring the user to log on once and then permit access to each of the authorized servers for that user.

A single logon approach should also ensure that the passwords are stored and transmitted securely. We call such a scheme *secure single logon*. Password security can be provided by implementing either a trusted third party or one-time passwords. For some environments, however, it may be desirable to implement a combination of the two approaches.

Requirements

For secure single logon, the security system must:

- Support a single logon by the user
- Provide access to each server that the user is authorized to use once they have logged on
- Coordinate and maintain the userID and password for each user and each server
- Provide secure storage and transport of passwords

Single Logon Sequence

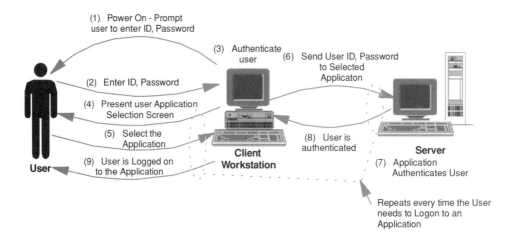

Figure 2.6: Basic Single Sign On Exchange

A hypothetical sequence for single logon is depicted in Figure 2.6. It consists of the following steps:

1. When the workstation is powered on, the user is prompted to enter the ID and the password.

2. The user enters the ID and the password.

3. The single logon code at the workstation authenticates the user by verifying the password for the ID. The single logon code may access a security server (not shown) to verify the user password for authentication.

4. The single logon code at the workstation presents the user with an application selection screen. This screen includes each application (or server) for which the user is authorized access.

5. The user selects the desired application.

6. The single logon code at the workstation sends the ID and the password to the selected application.

7. The application authenticates the ID and the password.

8. The application informs the client workstation that the user is authenticated.

9. The client workstation informs the user that logon is completed.

Once the first logon is completed, only steps 4 through 9 are executed every time the user desires to log on another application.

Single Logon Using One-Time Passwords

To address the security and productivity considerations for logon, it may be desirable to address the security concern by using one-time passwords and the productivity concerns by using the single logon. Such an approach would allow the use of one-time passwords for user authentication. The one-time passwords can be obtained by using the token cards described earlier. Alternatively, some vendors are offering software-generated one-time passwords. For example, IBM's Resource Access Control Facility (RACF) generates one-time passwords (IBMRACF 1993).

Authorization and Access Control

Authentication verifies the identity of users, whereas *access control* enforces the user *authorizations*. Consider a company's personnel file. The human resources manager should be permitted to read and write on the file. However, other employees should be permitted only to access their individual records. Furthermore, the company may not allow the employees to update some of the fields in their records. Although employees can change their home address or spouse name, they may not be permitted to modify the employee performance record or current salary. Access control mechanisms support different levels of authority and access to resources.

Access control mechanisms are often described in terms of three entities: *subjects*, *objects*, and *access rights*. A subject is an entity that can access an object. A subject can be a host, a user, or an application. An object is a resource to which access should be controlled. An object can range from a data field in a file to a large program.

Access rights specify the level of authority for a subject to access an object, so access rights are defined for each subject-object pair. Examples of access rights include *read*, *write*, and *execute*. The access right to write a file includes the authority to update the file. The access right to execute permits the user to execute a program or search a directory.

Access control is the mechanism that enforces access rights. *Authorization* is the process of assigning access rights to each subject.

The access control mechanism is implemented as part of the system services that process resource requests. It can be visualized by reviewing Figure 2.7. A user or an application program issues the OPEN command to access a resource. The command includes the userID. It also includes the file mode which refers to whether the resource is to be opened to process read, write, or execute operations. Upon receiving the OPEN request, the system code uses the *access control list (ACL)*, or some other access control mechanism, to obtain the access rights for the received userID. Next, the system code compares the user's access rights with the requested file mode. If there is a match, then the resource is opened; otherwise, an error message is returned to the OPEN request.

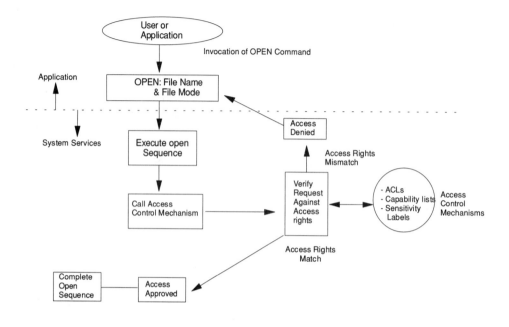

Figure 2.7: Access Control Design

Access rights can be assigned by the resource owner or the system administrator. There are certain trade-offs for each approach, as described next.

Discretionary Access Control

Discretionary access control (DAC) requires that each resource owner specify the access rights for all of its users. DAC is based on the premise that a resource owner is the best judge to determine the levels of access for its users. This approach has the benefit that it often provides open data sharing among users.

The primary drawback of this approach is that it lacks consistency across the enterprise. Every resource owner may not apply the same security policy in assigning the access rights. In particular, some resource owner may forget to implement adequate protection for the resources. DAC commonly is used where security is not the primary consideration. In such cases, the overriding objective is to provide flexible and open access to resources.

Mandatory Access Control

Mandatory access control (MAC) requires that the system administrator assign access rights to each user of each resource. In this way, a consistent security policy can be implemented across the network. MAC also makes it easy to enforce a strong security policy across all of the resources in the network. In my opinion, MAC schemes are not as flexible as DAC because MAC does not allow the resource owner to determine the level of access by its users. MAC schemes are particularly suited to situations where security is a primary consideration.

Given these pros and cons, it may be desirable for a company to implement a mixture of DAC and MAC schemes. The company may deploy DAC for the departmental or workgroup files, such as those used to share development tools among a group of programmers. However, for assigning access rights for files that contain confidential company-wide information such as plans and strategies, MAC scheme may be the right choice.

UNIX Permission

UNIX permissions specify access rights for UNIX files. There are three types of permissions for a UNIX file:

- Permission to read
- Permission to write, that is, to update the file
- Permission to execute, that is, to use the file as a program

These three permissions are assigned for three types of users. The three user types are:

- The owner
- Other users in the owner's user group
- All others

For example, assume I created a program that sorts the bibliography in alphabetic order. I should have the right to read, write, or execute the program. My (hypothetical) friend John helped me write and test the program. So he should have the rights to read and execute the program. I also allow other colleagues in my user group to read or execute this program. For all others, I want to permit access only to execute the file. So the UNIX permissions for my program will be:

$(rwx)\ (r-x)\ (--x)$

There are three entries for each user type. There is an entry each for read, write, and execute. A "-" implies that the corresponding right is not allowed. Additional details on UNIX permissions can be found in any UNIX book, such as Brown (1984). Additional information on access control can be found in Ahuja (1996), Shaffer (1994), and Amoroso (1994).

Covert Channels

Covert channels are unauthorized ways to exploit existing legitimate channels. For example, the name of a file or the availability versus unavailability of a resource can be used as a covert way to communicate secret information.

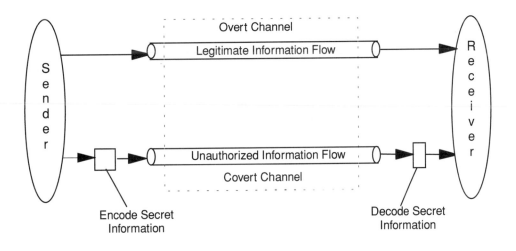

Figure 2.8: Overt and Covert Channels

Covert channels are used to transfer confidential information to unauthorized recipients, as shown in Figure 2.8. Covert channels exist 24 hours a day, 7 days a week. The confidential information may be covertly delivered in real time or stored for later access by the unauthorized recipient. Covert channels are often created to bypass MAC schemes, particularly when MAC is incorrectly implemented.

Covert channels are not easy to detect. Kemmerer (1983) describes an approach using a resource matrix to identify covert channels. Other references on this topic include Russell (1991), Shaffer (1994), Loepere (1985), Girling (1987), Kang (1995), and Browne (1995). Access control is also described in Abrams (1990) and Carson (1988).

Confidentiality

Data confidentiality provides the means to protect information from unauthorized disclosure. A user at a workstation may desire to send information to another user while ensuring that no one else can intercept and interpret the message. This requirement has existed for a very long time. In the early times, secret messages were sent from the battlegrounds to the home front. These messages were written in such a way that even if the messenger were caught, the message could not be interpreted. Mary, Queen of Scots, lost her life when the secret message she sent from her prison was intercepted and decoded. Encryption was also extensively used and attacked during the second World War.

Data confidentiality is achieved by encrypting the message at the sender and decrypting it at the receiver, as shown in Figure 2.9. *Encryption* consists of transforming the message in such a way that only the intended recipient can interpret it. The original data is called *plaintext*. The resulting data after applying the encryption algorithm is called the *encrypted data, ciphertext,* or *cipher.*

Decryption is the reverse process; it transforms the ciphertext to plaintext. The transformation is performed using one of several encryption algorithms and an encryption key. Although the encryption algorithms are published and available in various textbooks, the encryption key is divulged only to the sender and the receiver. In this way, only the receiver can interpret the encoded data. However, the encryption key should be securely transmitted to the receiver. So the process of confidentially transmitting a message consists of four steps:

- The sender encrypts the plaintext message using an algorithm and a secret key
- The sender transmits the encrypted message to the receiver
- The sender securely transmits the key to the receiver
- The receiver uses the encryption key to decrypt the message and obtains the plaintext message

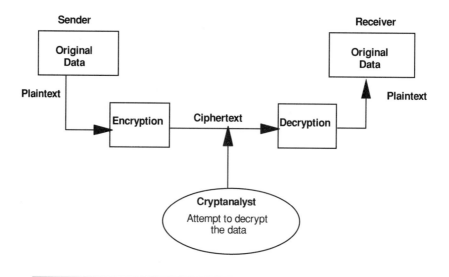

Figure 2.9: Encryption Process

The cryptographic algorithm is at the heart of providing confidentiality for user data. The cryptographic algorithm specifies ways to transform the original plaintext message into an uninterpretable text. Before proceeding to review some of the encryption algorithms, we introduce some concepts in cryptography. There are two basic techniques used in creating an encryption algorithm. The plaintext data can be encoded using transposition or substitution.

Transposition rearranges the order of the letters in the plaintext to make it difficult to recreate the plaintext. For example, the word ATTACK can be rearranged to KTAACT. This simple transposition can be the target of a brute-force attack. By attempting various arrangements, the original text can be recreated easily. Another approach is to use a *transposition matrix.* In a transposition matrix, the original text is written out a row at a time, until all of the text is entered. Then the text is written out a column at a time, thereby rendering the text incomprehensible for an intruder. The receiver recreates the transposition matrix and obtains the original text. To protect the data, the values of the number of rows and columns of the transposition matrix must be known only to the sender and the receiver. The transposition scheme is shown in Figure 2.10.

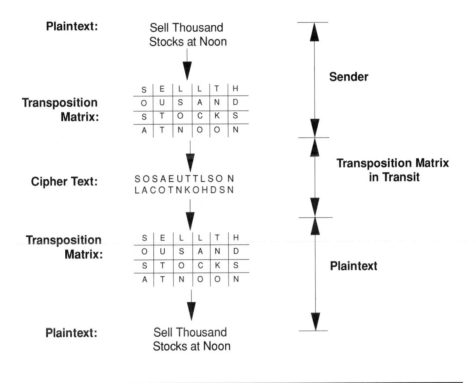

Figure 2.10: Transposition

Substitution implies replacing each letter by another letter in the alphabet. Consider the simple approach where each letter in the original text is replaced by the next letter in the alphabet. So, the word ATTACK would be replaced by the word BUUBDL.

These two techniques are the basic approaches to create encryption schemes. Although these techniques are simple and can be a convenient target of a successful brute-force attack, the current encryption algorithms are significantly more complex and cost more computing time for a brute-force attack. For details on brute-force attacks on cryptographic algorithms, see Schneier (1995).

The topic of cryptology addresses the various aspects of creating the encryption algorithms. A discussion on the details of the encryption schemes is beyond the scope of this book. However, we will review some of the common encryption algorithms. The strength of an encryption scheme depends on the algorithm and the length of the secret encryption key.

Data Encryption Standard (DES)

The *Data Encryption Standard (DES)* was originally developed by IBM in the 1970s. The National Bureau of Standards adapted DES and approved the new version in 1977 as the Data Encryption Standard. DES uses 56-bit encryption keys. The input data consists of a 64-bit block of plaintext; the output is 64 bits of encrypted text. The decryption process is similar to the encryption process. The same 56-bit encryption key is used for encryption and decryption. Details on the DES algorithm can be found in several books on security and cryptology, such as Stallings (1995), Schneier (1994), and Ahuja (1996).

DES is commonly used in the industry to protect data. Several vendors offer software products and hardware chips that provide DES encryption and decryption.

Triple-DES

Although DES has been widely accepted, there has been some concern about the strength of DES given its key length of only 56 bits. So an adaptation of the current DES algorithm has been developed. This adaptation does not require any changes to the existing DES software other than the additions to the DES code to allow multiple DES operations.

Triple-DES consists of executing three steps of DES encryption or decryption at the sender and at the receiver. The original text is processed three times through the DES process at the sender. At the receiver, the ciphertext is transformed through three iterations of DES process to obtain the original text.

At the sender, the plaintext is first encrypted using one key and the resulting output is decrypted using the second key. The output of this step is then encrypted using the third key and the resulting ciphertext is sent to the receiver. The receiver executes the DES algorithm exactly in the reverse order. So the receiver first decrypts the ciphertext using the third key, then encrypts using the second key, and finally decrypts using the first key. Triple-DES may be implemented using two or three keys. Common Triple-DES implementations use two 56-bit keys such as the one shown in Figure 2.11, although three 56-bit key implementations also exist. In either case, the result is a stronger encryption scheme than the basic DES algorithm.

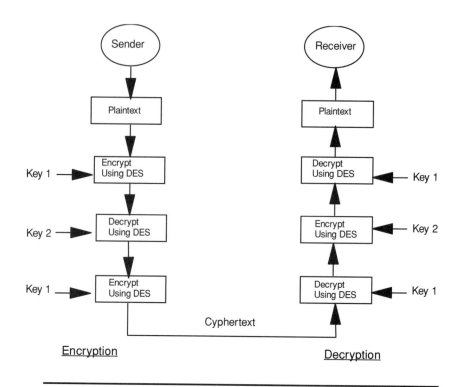

Figure 2.11: Triple DES Overview

Commercial Data Masking Facility (CDMF)

Commercial Data Masking Facility (CDMF) was developed by IBM. CDMF uses 40-bit encryption keys. As such, the algorithm strength is weaker than the 56-bit DES algorithm. According to Johnson (1994), products implementing CDMF algorithm in an appropriate manner, in general, may be freely exported from the United States. Details on CDMF can be found in Johnson (1994).

International Data Encryption Algorithm (IDEA)

International Data Encryption Algorithm (IDEA) was developed by the Swiss Federal Institute of Technology in 1991. This scheme uses 128-bit encryption keys, which implies it is stronger than the DES algorithm. This algorithm is relatively new, but is already used in PGP (see Chapter 3).

Among other algorithms, *RC2* and *RC4* are encryption schemes developed by Ron Rivest of RSA Data Security, Inc. According to RSA (1993), RC2 and RC4 are variable-key-size cipher functions designed for bulk encryption. Since these algorithms support variable key size, they can be made more secure than DES by using key sizes longer than 56 bits. They can also be less secure than DES by using short key sizes. The public key cryptography is described in Chapter 5.

Cryptographic algorithms, such as DES, can operate in one of several modes. These modes specify the way in which data is handled for encryption. For example, the *Cipher Block Chaining (CBC) Mode* modifies the algorithms so that the same 64-bit plaintext will generate different ciphertext every time. Details on these modes as well as the general topic of cryptography can be found in IBMDATAS (1977), Stallings (1995), Schneier (1994), and Diffie (1976).

Data Integrity

Data integrity prevents unauthorized modifications of information. It is often used to ensure that no unauthorized individual has modified the data since it originated at the sender or since it was last stored in the file.

Data integrity is not the same as data confidentiality. Data confidentiality protects data from disclosure to unauthorized users. On the other hand, data integrity ensures that the data has not been tampered with, while it does not prevent other users from interpreting the data.

The concept of data integrity is not new, although its use has changed. In the early 1970s, digital data was transmitted over analog lines. Analog lines generally have a higher rate of transmission errors than that for digital circuits. So to detect any transmission errors, the data link protocols included an error-detection scheme. The sender computed a number, called a *check sum*, by performing certain operations on the entire message. Then the message was transmitted along with the check sum. The receiver performed the same operation on the message and computed a new check sum. Next, the receiver compared its own check sum with that received from the sender. A match in the two numbers assured the receiver that there were no errors during transmission.

The current data integrity algorithms use a similar concept but with a higher level of security. The check sum is also called the *message digest, data integrity check,* and *message integrity check.* We use the term *message digest* in this book unless otherwise stated. The message digest is computed by applying a one-way hash function on the input data block. A one-way hash function produces the message digest so that it is very hard to obtain the original data block from the message digest. The process to verify data integrity is depicted in Figure 2.12. We briefly review some of the message digest algorithms.

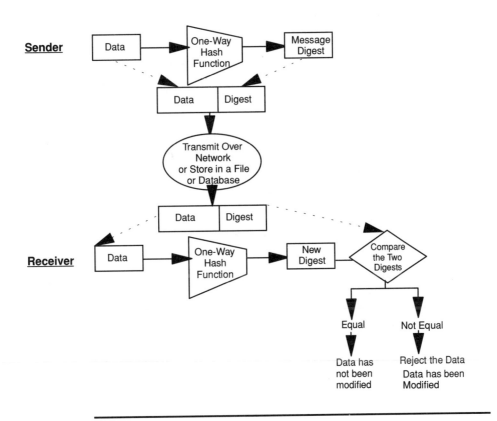

Figure 2.12: Data Integrity Using One-Way Hash Function

Message Digest Algorithms

The strength of a message digest algorithm is reflected by the algorithm and the size of the message digest. Typical message digest sizes are 128 bits and 160 bits.

There are two classes of common message digest algorithms. First, Rivest designed Message Digest 2 (MD2), improved it with Message Digest 4 (MD4), and then improved it again with the Message Digest 5 (MD5) algorithm. The MD4 algorithm is described in RFC 1320 (Rivest 1992b) and the MD5 algorithm is documented in RFC 1321 (Rivest 1992a). Each of these algorithms accept messages of arbitrary lengths and generate a 128-bit message digest.

The National Institute of Standards and Technology (NIST) developed another class of message digest algorithms. Secure Hash Algorithm (SHA) generates a 160-bit message digest. It was published as a federal standard in 1993.

Schneier (1995) provides computational requirements to launch brute-force attacks against these algorithms.

The message digest is computed using a secret key that is shared between the sender and the receiver. Thus the sender is authenticated to the receiver. Although this scheme protects the sender and receiver from a third party, it does not protect the sender and the receiver from each other. For example, Tom and Lucy share the secret key to compute the message authentication code. So, Tom creates a message and appends the message authentication code using the shared key. Now Tom can claim that this message came from Lucy. Similarly, Lucy can create a message, append the authentication code using the shared key, and claim that it came from Tom.

To address this lack of trust between two parties, the message digest (or the authentication code) should be encrypted using the private key of the sender. Since this private key is known only to the sender, the receiver can claim that the message indeed came from the sender. The Public Key system is described in Chapter 5.

Security APIs

Generic Security Service API (GSSAPI)

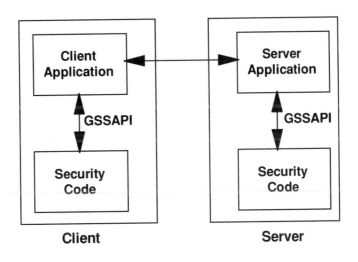

Figure 2.13: GSSAPI Usage

Generic Security Service Application Program Interface (GSSAPI) is the first application program interface to provide a general-purpose interface for security services. It was approved in 1993 by the Internet Engineering Task Force (IETF) and published as RFC 1508 (Linn 1993b) and 1509 (Wray 1993). The use of GSSAPI is depicted in Figure 2.13. An application residing at the client workstation accesses security services by issuing a GSSAPI call. The call is processed and responded to by the security code at the client workstation. The client application communicates directly with the server application over the network.

For example, suppose the client application needs to send an encrypted message to the server. The client application calls the security code at the client workstation by issuing a GSSAPI (called GSS_SEAL) to the security code. The call includes the message to be encrypted. The security code returns an encrypted message to the client application, and the client application sends the encrypted message to the server application. The server application issues another GSSAPI call (GSS_UNSEAL) to the security code at the server, the security code decrypts the message and returns the plaintext message to the server application.

The GSSAPI is independent of the underlying security schemes. As such, the same calls will work for any type of underlying encryption scheme.

Generic Cryptographic Service API (GCSAPI)

X/Open intends to publish a preliminary specifications of this API. According to IBMEWS (1995), it should include the following cryptographic services: creation and verification of message integrity check, encryption and decryption, generating irreversible hash of data and random numbers. It should also include key management services such as generating, deriving, and deleting keys; export and import of keys; and storage, archival, and retrieval of keys.

Generic Audit Service API (GASAPI)

According to IBMEWS (1995), requirements for this API include support of standalone and distributed systems, defining the data to be recorded, format for security event messages, and support for confidentiality and data integrity.

Cryptography Export from United States

The topic of export regulations for cryptographic products is addressed by Schneier (1995, 95), RSA (1993), and Russell (1991, 198–199). We briefly describe this topic based on these three references.

The U.S. government treats cryptography as a weapon. As such it is covered under the same export regulations as those for military weapons. The rules are specified by the Department of State, Office of Defense Trade Controls, in the document called International Traffic in Arms Regulations (ITAR), as stated in Schneier (1995, 95). To export a cryptographic product outside the United States (or to a "foreign person" inside the United States), an appropriate export licence is required from the Office of Munitions Control (OMC) of the Department of State, according to Russell (1991, 198).

Russell also states that DES products can be sold without restrictions to any organization that is located in the United States and is U.S. owned and controlled. However, these products can be exported only with an appropriate licence.

According to Schneier (1995, 95) and RSA (1993, 37), special provisions have been made to allow export of RC2 and RC4 algorithms provided that the key lengths are 40 bits or less.

According to RSA (1993), a vendor seeking to export a product using cryptography first submits a request to the State Department's Defense Trade Control Office. Export jurisdiction may then be passed to the Department of Commerce. The National Security Agency (NSA) has *de facto* control over export of cryptographic products. NSA's stated policy is not to restrict export when cryptography is used for authentication; it is only concerned with the use of cryptography for confidentiality. So a vendor seeking export of a product that uses cryptography for authentication will be permitted only if the vendor can demonstrate that the product cannot be easily adapted for use of data encryption.

Over the last few years, the U.S. government has brought forth proposals such as the clipper and the key escrow schemes. The key escrow scheme uses public key technology, which is addressed in Chapter 5. Finally, the cryptography export policy is under constant review and may lead to changes over time.

Internet Security

"Security exposures are like car problems. Ignoring them won't fix it."

Internet security means "peace-of-mind" for corporate America.

Internet security ensures that the users can communicate over the Internet without the fear of theft, interception, or break-in. To secure the applications and data transmission over the Internet, several security mechanisms have emerged over the last few years. The Appendices provide an overview of TCP/IP and the World Wide Web. In the preceding chapters, we have presented the risks to networks, and concepts in network security. For this chapter, our goal is to review the mechanisms that secure the TCP/IP and Internet components.

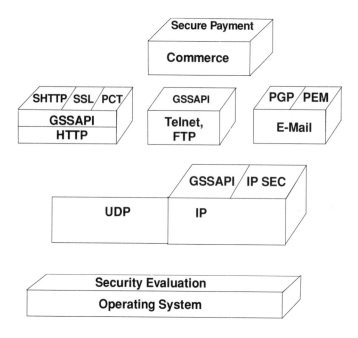

Figure 3.1: Internet Security

Figure 3.1 depicts some of the main components of an Internet host that supports the Web and electronic commerce. Starting from the bottom, the operating system must be based on a secure design. Security evaluations of operating systems are critical to their acceptance as secure operating systems, as described later.

The IP layer can be secured by the recently introduced set of IP Security standards. The IP Security standards specify security services for the IP layer. As a result, the TCP/IP applications can access the security services through the IP layer. Next, electronic mail (e-mail) can be secured by implementing one of the secure e-mail schemes. These schemes, called Privacy

Enhanced Mail (PEM) and Pretty Good Privacy (PGP), provide a variety of security services for the e-mail.

Most of the software components can access security services such as data confidentiality and data integrity by issuing calls to a security interface. For example, TELNET and FTP software can be upgraded to utilize the Generic Security Service Application Program Interface (GSSAPI) (the GSSAPI was introduced in Chapter 2). In this chapter, we will review the following security topics or schemes:

- Secure Operating Systems

- Secure IP

- Secure e-mail
  Pretty Good Privacy
  Privacy Enhanced Mail

- Secure TELNET

As shown in Figure 3.1, additional security mechanisms are required to protect business transactions on the Internet. These schemes address security for the World Wide Web and the electronic commerce. We will present these schemes in Chapters 6, 7 and 8.

Secure Operating Systems

Network security relies on a secure underlying operating system. Any security scheme protecting the Internet must utilize a variety of system services such as access control to its files, access rights for the users, sensitivity labels[*] for the file records, and system integrity. On the other hand, an insecure operating system can expose its resources to penetration from intruders.

In Chapter 2, we discussed the topics of passwords and access control. User passwords must be stored in a secure fashion. Secured password storage includes encrypting passwords before storage (such as in a UNIX system) and restricted access to the password file. If the operating system does not provide support for such features, then passwords can be stolen. As stated earlier, a stolen password can expose the security of all the resources accessible through that password.

There has been a renewed focus on ensuring security for the operating systems. Several countries have defined a criteria to the security of the operating systems.

The U. S. Department of Defense published *Trusted Computer Systems Evaluation Criteria (TCSEC)* in 1985. TCSEC defines a rating scale by specifying four divisions of secure systems, division A, B, C, and D. Division D refers to the most insecure systems and division A specifies the most secure systems. Each division specifies a variety of requirements that must be satisfied; we briefly describe some of them.

Division D specifies minimal protection. Division C requires identification and authentication, discretionary access control (DAC), audit, and object reuse. Division B requirements include all of division C requirements plus sensitivity labels, mandatory access control (MAC), and covert channel analysis. Division A requirements include all of division B requirements plus formal design specification and verification, and covert channel analysis. Each division, in turn, includes one or more

---

* Sensitivity labels are assigned to define the security level and the type of information under that security level. Decision to access a file is based on the labels of the subject and the object.

hierarchical classes. In all, there are a total of seven classes in TCSEC. TCSEC is described in Chokhani (1992), Ahuja (1996), and Russell (1991).

The European Community has published *Information Technology Security Evaluation Criteria (ITSEC)*. ITSEC also specifies seven levels that roughly correspond to the seven classes of TCSEC. ITSEC is described in ITSEC (1991).

Secure IP

In the last few years, the Internet standards community has focused on specifying security services for the IP layer. By providing security at the IP layer, any higher level application or protocol can access these services directly or indirectly. A set of five RFCs has been issued by the Internet Engineering Task Force (IETF). The RFCs, Atkinson (1995a RFC 1825), Atkinson (1995b RFC 1826), Atkinson (1995c RFC 1827), Metzger (1995 RFC 1828), and Karn (1995 RFC 1829), specify various aspects of IP layer security.

RFC 1825 describes the security mechanisms for IP version 4 (IPv4) and IP version 6 (IPv6). These mechanisms specify security for the IP layer only and do not address the overall security for the Internet. The *IP security* is provided through two schemes, the *IP Authentication Header (IP AH)* and the *IP Encapsulating Security Payload (IP ESP)*. The IP Authentication Header provides data integrity and authentication but no confidentiality. The IP ESP always provides confidentiality. Depending on the algorithm and the mode (described later), IP ESP may also support data integrity and authentication. The two schemes can be used separately or together.

Security Association

A *security association* provides the underlying correspondence for the use of security mechanisms between two communicating entities. The security association is used for the Authentication Header and the Encapsulating Security Payload. A particular security association is uniquely identified by the *Security Parameter Index (SPI)* and the destination address. The SPI is a 32-bit pseudo-random number. The sending host selects the SPI value based on the userID and the destination address. The receiving host uses the SPI value and the destination address to verify that the security association is correct. A security association is usually a one-way relationship. It normally consists of the following parameters, although additional parameters also may be supported.

- The authentication algorithm and the algorithm mode used for providing the authentication to IP AH. Keys used with the authentication algorithm.

- The algorithm and mode used to provide encryption for the ESP. Keys used with the encryption algorithm.

- The size and presence/absence of the encryption algorithm synchronization or initialization vector. This information relates to the encryption algorithm (not described here) and is required for IP ESP.

- The authentication algorithm used for the IP ESP transform, if any is in use. Keys used for this authentication algorithm.

- The lifetimes of the keys and the security association.

- The source address of the security association. In the event that more than one host share the same security association, this may be a wild card address.

• The sensitivity level of the secured data such as CONFIDENTIAL, SECRET, and UNCLASSIFIED. This parameter is required if the host claims multi-level security support.

IP Authentication Header

As stated, the *IP Authentication Header (IP AH)* provides authentication and data integrity but no confidentiality. Since the IP AH does not provide confidentiality, it can be used across various countries on the Internet without being impacted by export restrictions for the cryptographic algorithms. Furthermore, many encryption algorithms, when implemented in software, may impact the overall performance and the end-to-end delay in transmitting a packet. As such, IP AH is expected to gain wide acceptance for Internet security services.

The IP Authentication Header provides security between any two or more hosts or gateways that support IP AH. A *gateway* simply provides communication between hosts on a trusted private network and untrusted public network such as the Internet. Firewall is an example of a gateway that we will describe in Chapter 4.

According to Atkinson (1995b RFC 1826), any IP AH compliant implementation must support keyed MD5 mechanism (see *Message Digest Algorithm*, Chapter 2). The 128-bit digest is computed based on RFC 1321 (Rivest 1992a). For IPv6, every host must support MD5 with a 128-bit key, according to Atkinson (1995a RFC 1825 p8). For IPv4, any host that claims support for IP AH must support MD5 with a 128-bit key. A host that supports IP AH can optionally support other authentication algorithms in addition to MD5.

For an IPv4 datagram, the IP authentication header is located between the IP header and the upper layer protocols such as TCP or UDP. For IPv6, there may be some additional fields that are not required for IPv4. In effect, the authentication header is located after all those fields that are examined at an intermediate hop. The Internet Assigned Number Authority has assigned port number 51 for IP AH. So the header immediately preceding the AH should include the number 51 in its next header field.

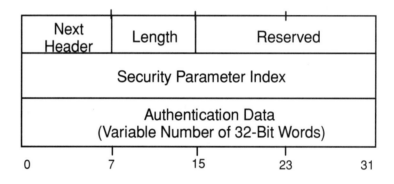

Figure 3.2: Authentication Header Format

The format of the Authentication Header is shown in Figure 3.2. The Next Header field is 8 bits long and identifies the data after the authentication payload. The Payload Length is also 8 bits; it provides the length of the authentication data field in 32-bit words. There are 16-bits reserved for future use. This field is ignored except that it is included in the authentication data calculation described below. So these bits must be set to zero.

The Security Parameter Index (SPI), as described earlier, is a 32-bit pseudo-random binary number that identifies the security association. A value of 0 implies that no security association exists. The SPI values of 1 through 255 are reserved for future use.

The authentication data has a variable length, but it is always an integral number of 32-bit words. The authentication data is calculated using a message digest algorithm. RFC 1826 (Atkinson 1995b) states that only those algorithms that are believed to be cryptographically strong one-way functions should be used. Conventional check sum algorithms such as CRC-16 are not cryptographically strong. As such, CRC-16 must not be used to compute the authentication data.

IP Encapsulating Security Payload

IP ESP always provides confidentiality, and it can optionally provide data integrity and authentication. IP ESP encapsulates either the entire datagram or only the header portion of the upper layer protocols such as TCP, UDP, or ICMP. It encrypts most of the content inside the encapsulated portion and appends a plaintext header at the end. It is this plaintext header that is used to route the packet through the network.

The ESP payload appears between the IP Header and the transport level protocol. The Internet Assigned Number Authority has assigned protocol number 50 for ESP. So, the header immediately preceding ESP should include the number 50 in the next header field. ESP consists of an unencrypted header and an encrypted data field. The encrypted data field may include the protected ESP header fields and the protected user data, which is the entire datagram or simply the upper-level protocol packet.

According to RFC 1825 (Atkinson 1995a p10), a host that supports IP ESP must support DES in CBC (Cipher Block Chaining) mode. Support of other encryption algorithms or modes is optional. This requirement also imposes constraints due to export restrictions because algorithms with no more than 40-bit encryption keys can be considered for export.

IP ESP encrypts most of the ESP contents and appends a new plaintext IP header to be used for routing through the network. Similar to IP AH, IP ESP works between two or more hosts and security gateways.

Hosts that implement the Encapsulating Security Payload may experience some performance impact. First, there is the additional processing required for handling the ESP protocols at the sending and the receiving hosts. Secondly, the sending host and the receiving host will also expend processor time to perform encryption and decryption respectively. This additional processing is often directly proportional to the size of the packet and can increase the total time (also called the *latency*) to transfer a packet between two IP layers. The actual performance impact depends on the specific processor and the ESP implementation. In certain cases, it may be preferable to incorporate appropriate additional hardware that encrypts/decrypts the data units.

Tunnel-Mode

ESP can operate in Tunnel-mode or Transport-mode. In *Tunnel-mode*, ESP encapsulates the complete datagram. In *Transport-mode*, only an upper-level protocol, such as TCP or UDP data is encapsulated. This mode conserves the bandwidth since there are no encrypted IP headers.

For tunnel-mode, the ESP header is located following the end-to-end headers and immediately precedes the tunneled IP datagram. To send an ESP tunnel-mode datagram, the sender first encapsulates the original IP datagram. Next, it uses the userID and the destination address to obtain the appropriate security association. The sender uses information in the security association to encrypt the IP datagram. This encrypted ESP is encapsulated in a cleartext IP datagram. The receiving host strips off the cleartext IP header, obtains the SPI value from the received ESP header, and selects the appropriate security association using the destination address and the SPI value. Next, it uses the key in the security association to decrypt the received encrypted datagram.

Transport-Mode

In transport-mode, the ESP header is inserted immediately preceding the transport layer protocol header. As such, this mode preserves the bandwidth since there are no encrypted IP headers.

For transport-mode, the sending host first selects the transport layer datagram from the entire packet and encapsulates it in ESP. Next, the sending host obtains the security association using the userID and the destination address and applies the cryptographic algorithm to encrypt the transport level datagram. This encrypted ESP is included as the last field of a cleartext IP datagram. The receiver processes the IP headers and obtains the SPI value from the ESP headers. Next, it uses the destination address and the SPI value to obtain the security association, acquires the encryption information from the security association, and uses the cryptographic algorithm to decrypt the encrypted ESP payload.

Key Management

The key management for IP Security is not yet defined by the Internet Engineering Task Force (IETF). The key management protocol will specify ways to establish and distribute keys through several hosts that implement IP security. For a few hosts, the keys may be manually distributed through offline methods such as secure mail or a phone call. However, formal protocols are required for key distribution among a large number of hosts or networks with frequent additions or removals of hosts.

IP Security Usage

IP Security is gaining momentum given its applicability across various operating system and its implementation below the TCP application layer protocols. Several firewall vendors have implemented IP security and have also established interoperability with other vendors. Some of the implementations of IP security can be used to create a secure private network, as described next.

Virtual Private Networks

A *Virtual Private Network* consists of a collection of hosts that have implemented protocols to securely exchange information. Often, these hosts communicate over the Internet or some other public network. However, a virtual private network can also be created within a private network. For example, the military may define a highly secure virtual private network that is defined within its private network.

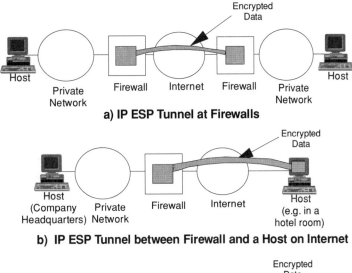

a) IP ESP Tunnel at Firewalls

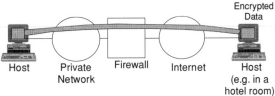

b) IP ESP Tunnel between Firewall and a Host on Internet

c) IP ESP Tunnel between a Host on the Private Network and a Host on the Internet

Figure 3.3: Virtual Private Networks: Use of IP ESP Tunnel in Hosts and Firewalls

Figure 3.3 depicts the concept of a virtual private network. Each participating host has implemented the IP Security. IP AH is implemented if only data integrity and authentication are required. If confidentiality is also required, then IP ESP is implemented. As a result, each host can securely communicate with other hosts.

It should be noted that IP AH or IP ESP can be implemented at the gateways, the hosts, or both. When it is implemented only at the gateways, it provides secure communication over the untrusted public network. When IP AH or IP ESP is implemented at the hosts, it provides secure communications between the two hosts at the endpoints. Whereas the firewall protects the private network from external intrusions, the IP security at the hosts provides end-to-end security. As such, the two schemes complement each other and can be used together as shown in Figure 3.3.

This description is based on information contained in several RFCs. RFC 1825 (Atkinson 1995a) describes the overall architecture for IP layer security and provides an informative overview of the approaches. RFC 1826 (Atkinson 1995b) provides details on IP Authentication Header, and RFC 1827 (Atkinson 1995c) provides description of IP Encapsulating Security Payload. RFC 1828 (Metzger 1995) presents the use of MD5 for authentication and RFC 1829 (Karn 1995) describes the ESP DES-CBC transforms.

Secure E-Mail

Electronic mail (e-mail) requires security to protect its contents and to ensure message authentication. Security requirements for e-mail should also provide for privacy so that no unauthorized disclosures occur during transmission. Requirements for e-mail security are:

- Confidentiality: to prevent the message from being disclosed to anyone not authorized to receive it. This requirement also addresses attacks such as wiretaps or erroneous delivery of messages to unauthorized receivers.

- Data Origin Authentication: to reliably ensure the origin of the message. This requirement addresses attacks where an intruder modifies the source of the message.

- Message Integrity: to ensure that the contents of the message have not been tampered by unauthorized means since the message left the sender.

- Nonrepudiation: to protect a recipient against the false denial of a sender that the data was sent. It should also protect a sender against the false denial by a recipient that the data was received. Nonrepudiation is described in detail in Chapter 5.

In the last few years, two primary schemes have emerged that directly address these security requirements for e-mail: Privacy Enhanced Mail (PEM) and Pretty Good Privacy (PGP).

Privacy Enhanced Mail (PEM)

In 1985, the Internet Architecture Board initiated the secure e-mail project under its Privacy and Security Research Group (PSRG). A series of Request for Comments (RFCs) were issued by the Internet Engineering Task Force (IETF) as a result of the work under the PEM Working Group. RFC 1421 (Linn 1993a), RFC 1422 (Kent 1993a), RFC 1423 (Balenson 1993), and RFC

1424 (Kalisky 1993) provide the basis for creating a secure e-mail over the Internet. In addition, Kent (1993b) and Schneier (1995) provide a good description of the PEM system. We use mainly these references for the following description.

Security Services

Every PEM message provides authentication, data integrity, and nonrepudiation. Confidentiality is an optional feature for PEM messages.

Message Types

PEM specifies three types of messages that offer combinations of cryptographic services.

- MIC-CLEAR
- MIC-ONLY
- ENCRYPTED

A *MIC-CLEAR* message provides data integrity and authentication by using a *Message Integrity Check (MIC)*. A MIC-CLEAR message does not provide confidentiality and encoding. By excluding the coding step, a MIC-CLEAR message can be "read" by hosts that do not support PEM. A PEM host can verify the integrity and authenticity of a MIC-CLEAR message. A non-PEM host can view the message but not verify the integrity or the authenticity. As such, a MIC-CLEAR message can be used for a mailing list that consists of a mix of PEM and non-PEM capable hosts.

A *MIC-ONLY* message includes the security functions of MIC-CLEAR plus an encoding step. This encoding step ensures that a PEM message can be passed through various e-mail gateways without being transformed in such a way as to invalidate the message integrity check.

An *ENCRYPTED* message provides the services of a MIC-ONLY message plus confidentiality. So, in effect, an ENCRYPTED message provides confidentiality, message integrity, and authenticity. An ENCRYPTED message also includes the encoding step that is specified for MIC-ONLY messages. For confidentiality, an ENCRYPTED message is encrypted before transmission and decrypted at the destination host.

Message Transmission

PEM message processing consists of four steps:

1. Canonicalization
2. Message integrity and digital signature
3. Optional Encryption
4. Optional transmission encoding

A MIC-CLEAR message executes steps 1 and 2; a MIC-ONLY message processes steps 1, 2, and 4; and an ENCRYPTED message follows steps 1 through 4.

Canonicalization

PEM converts each message to a standard format. In this way, the message can be received and interpreted by the receiver even though the sending host and the receiving host may have different operating systems. Without canonicalization, every host will have to implement translation to every other type of host system.

PEM applies format conversion before the message is encrypted. In this way, the format conversion does not impact the encryption and message integrity check. Note that a format conversion after the message integrity check computation may invalidate the message integrity.

Message Integrity and Digital Signature

PEM specifies the use of RSA and MD2 or MD5 for message integrity algorithms. The MIC is signed by the originator to avoid an attack where an intruder can change the source identity in the message. The receiver also requires verification of the claimed identity of the sender. In order to permit that, the sender includes its X.509 certificate with the message. X.509 certificates are described in Chapter 5.

Data Encryption

PEM allows optional encryption of a message. It specifies the use of DES in Cipher Block Chaining (CBC) mode for the cryptographic algorithm. This step is executed only if the message type is ENCRYPTED.

Details on various cryptographic algorithms including the message integrity algorithms are specified in RFC 1423 (Balenson 1993).

Encoding

This step is executed only if the message type is MIC-ONLY or ENCRYPTED. PEM converts the message into a text using 6-bit alphabet. This encoding is compatible with the SMTP (Simple Message Transfer Protocol) canonicalization format.

Receiving a PEM Message

The receiving host first checks the message type. If the message type is MIC-ONLY or ENCRYPTED, then the message is decoded. If it is an ENCRYPTED message, then PEM first inverts the 6-bit text to 8-bit ciphertext. If the message is not ENCRYPTED, then the 6-bit encoding is transformed to canonical plaintext. Next, the message is decrypted if the message type in ENCRYPTED. Now the processing is common for a MIC-ONLY or MIC-CLEAR message. First, the message integrity and authenticity is checked using the MIC algorithm and the signature algorithm. Finally, the canonical format is transformed into a format that is compatible with the receiving host.

Certificate Usage

The use of X.509 certificates in PEM is described in Chapter 5.

Pretty Good Privacy (PGP)

Pretty Good Privacy (PGP) is a product that secures the e-mail traffic. In contrast to PEM, PGP is not a standard and does not interoperate with PEM or any other scheme. PGP version 1 was designed and developed by Philip Zimmermann in June 1991. The current version of PGP is 2.6.2 and 2.7. ViaCrypt sells PGP version 2.7 for commercial use. It is available free of charge on the Internet.

Security Services

PGP provides the following security services for e-mail: confidentiality, data origin authentication, data integrity, and origin nonrepudiation.

Confidentiality ensures that the contents of the message are not revealed to an unauthorized recipient. PGP provides confidentiality by encrypting the message using IDEA algorithm in Cipher Block Chaining mode (see Chapter 2). IDEA uses 128-bit encryption keys.

Data origin authentication assures the recipient about the identity of the sender. Message integrity provides the assurance that the message has not been tampered during transmission since it left the sender. Data origin authentication and message integrity are accomplished in two steps. First, a one-way hash function is applied to the message and the resulting message digest is appended to the message. Next, the message digest is encrypted by the private key (see Chapter 5) that is available only to the sender. The receiver uses the sender's public key to decrypt the message, which ensures that the digest was indeed encrypted by the identified sender of the message. PGP uses

MD5 and RSA algorithms for data integrity and source authentication. PGP's RSA keys come in three sizes: 384 bits, 512 bits, and 1024 bits. Key size of 384 bits should be used only for testing; 1024-bit keys are considered secure, according to Schneier (1995 136).

PGP automatically provides confidentiality, authentication, and data integrity. However, it is possible to send a PGP message without confidentiality. PGP also allows a message to be sent without authentication or integrity.

PGP has certain unique attributes. First, PGP can be used to secure e-mail as well as to encrypt files. It offers an option to encrypt a file using IDEA algorithm. The second attribute relates to digital signatures. Conventionally, digital signatures are appended to the message. However, PGP allows the digital signature to be detached and transmitted separately from the message. There are certain advantages in providing detached digital signatures. For example, the digital signatures can be recorded and logged separately. In this way, the sender or the receiver can record all the messages that were sent or received. Another attribute of PGP is that it compresses messages using the commonly available ZIP 2.0 program. Compression reduces the size of the message and removes redundancies in the plaintext message. As a result, it makes the cryptanalysis task more difficult. Finally, as stated earlier, PGP is a software product. In contrast, PEM and other schemes described here are mostly the standards. Also, compared to PEM, PGP uses a different model for trust as described in Chapter 5.

Certificate Usage

The use of X.509 certificates in PGP is described in Chapter 5.

PGP is described in Schneier (1995) and Zimmermann (1995).

Secure TELNET

A TCP/IP application protocol can be treated as an application accessing security services. Then, the TCP/IP protocols, such as TELNET or FTP, can authenticate the clients, securely transmit the passwords, and provide encryption and data integrity services. The security services may be accessed using GSSAPI, as described in Chapter 2. This approach is depicted in Figure 3.4.

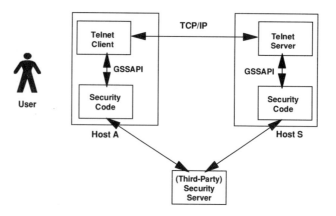

Figure 3.4: Secured Telnet

For example, consider that a user needs to access TELNET protocol. We assume that the network implementation includes GSSAPI to access security services, along with some third party authentication schemes.

1. The user at host A logs on the security server and obtains authentication information. This is the only user logon required for access to various applications, including TELNET. (To achieve this single logon, each participating TCP/IP application must implement GSSAPI calls for security services.)

2. The user wishes to establish a TELNET session with a server at host S, so the user enters the TELNET command along with the host name S.

3. The underlying security client code sends the user credentials (authentication information) to the server host S.

4. Assume that the server at host S has already been authenticated to the security server. Then the server accepts the user credentials and a TELNET session is established between the TELNET client and the server.

This approach can be extended to secure other Internet applications.

Internet Firewalls

4

As the size of the Internet grows, so do the risks to private networks attached to the Internet. To protect private networks from eavesdropping, intrusion, and other attacks from the Internet, an adequate barrier is required. This barrier, called a *firewall*, should intercept all the traffic between a given private network and the Internet. It should not only protect the company resources from hackers on the Internet, but should also intercept any transmission of valuable company information from the private network to the Internet.

To describe the topic of firewalls, we must review the concepts and functions of firewalls. Next, we describe each component of a firewall, namely the filters, proxy servers, domain name service, and mail handling.

Concepts

Firewalls

A *firewall* provides controlled access between a private network and the Internet. It intercepts each message between the private network and the Internet. Depending on the configuration, the firewall determines whether a data packet or a connection request should be permitted to pass through the firewall or be discarded. Figure 4.1 depicts the purpose of firewalls. In describing the firewalls, we will refer to two types of host systems. First, there are host systems on a secure, private, and trusted network. These host systems can access the Internet through a firewall. The other host systems are those that reside on the Internet, and can be accessed only through the untrusted Internet.

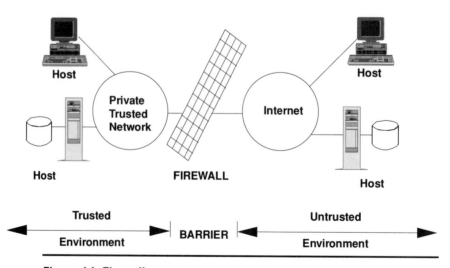

Figure 4.1: Firewall

Need for a Firewall

In the preceding chapters, several approaches were presented to protect networks. In particular, we described several schemes to secure TCP/IP and Internet services such as secure e-mail. Here we address the relationship of these Internet security schemes with firewalls.

A secure e-mail protects communications between two Internet users. IP Security, described in Chapter 3, protects communications at the IP layer. Later, we will also present schemes to protect communications among Web clients and servers. However, none of these approaches protect resources of a private network from attacks over the Internet. A firewall is similar to locking the doors of a house or employing a doorperson. The objective is to ensure that only the authorized people can enter the house, in addition to locking the bedroom closet that contains jewelry.

When a private network is attached to the Internet, there are three areas of potentials concerns or risks:

1. **Information**: someone can steal or destroy the information that is stored on the private network

2. **Resources**: someone can damage or misuse the computer systems on the private network

3. **Reputation**: someone can damage the reputation of a business by demonstrating vulnerabilities in its network security

There is an additional business need for firewalls. A company may desire to isolate access among the networks of different parts of its business. A university may require that the administrative network (where all student grades are stored) should be isolated from the students' computer network. Hospitals may want to keep the patient-records network separate from its administrative network for legal and ethical aspects of patient privacy. Such an intracompany protection can be provided by a firewall. This concept of a department-level firewall is shown in Figure 4.2. One or more firewalls may be used to provide isolation and controlled access between different parts of a company, as shown in Figure 4.2. Such firewalls are also called Intracompany or Intranet Firewalls.

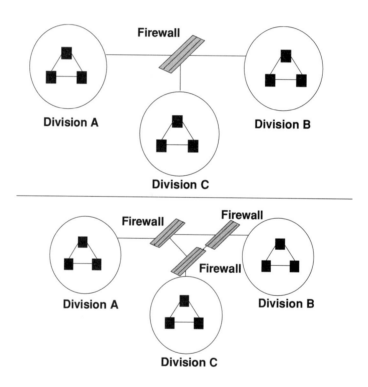

Figure 4.2: Firewall Usage for Intranet Security

Therefore a firewall is a software component that controls access between a private network and the Internet, or among different parts of a given private network. A firewall should satisfy the following requirements.

1. Any packet that is not explicitly permitted should default to a denial. This requirement implies that the administrator should explicitly specify the legitimate traffic that is allowed through the firewall. All other traffic, by default, should be rejected.

2. Wherever possible, keep outside users outside the private network. This requirement states that access from outside users into the private network should be restricted. If there is a need for Internet users to have open access to some files (such as a company's public files), then those files should be located outside the firewall and on the Internet side (see Figure 4.7).

3. Enforce extensive logging, auditing and alarm generation. This requirement means that the firewall should be capable of logging and auditing the traffic passing through the firewall. The firewall should also generate alarms when it suspects that someone is attempting to break into the firewall.

Firewall Design

A firewall design consists of several components. These components, depicted in Figure 4.3, are divided into five groups: secure operating system, filters, gateways, domain name service, and e-mail handling. We review these components next; the details are presented later in this chapter.

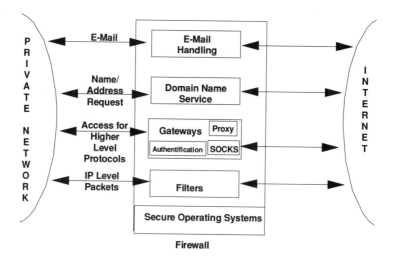

Figure 4.3: Components of a Firewall

First, the firewall must be located in a secure environment by residing on a secure operating system. A secure operating system can protect the firewall code and files from attacks by intruders. Often, the firewall code is the only application permitted to execute on a given host system. Absence of other applications on the firewall system reduces the possibility of unauthorized attempts to penetrate the firewall.

The Internet community often uses the term bastion host to refer to a firewall host. A **bastion host** is a highly secure computer since it is exposed to direct attacks from the hackers on the Internet. The term *bastion* comes from the heavily fortified projections on the exteriors of castles in medieval times.

Next, we introduce the concept of *filters*. The primary purpose of a firewall is to intercept the packets and permit only authorized traffic through the firewall. So, the firewall intercepts each packet that is transmitted between the private network and the Internet. The filter executes a set of rules that have been defined by the firewall administrator at configuration time. These rules are based on a variety of parameters including the IP addresses, the port numbers, and the type of application. The primary concern for the filters approach is that it is based on IP addresses, which in themselves are not secure. Since the IP addresses are not protected, a given host can spoof another host by changing the IP source address. The Source Address Spoofing attack, described in Chapter 1, exploits this weakness. Filters are described in detail later in this chapter.

An *application gateway* intercepts the traffic and authenticates users at the TCP/IP application level. The application gateway function is often provided by implementing a *proxy server*. A user on the private network logs on a proxy server. The proxy server authenticates the user and checks whether the user should be permitted to access the Internet. If all these checks are successful, then the user is permitted to log on the remote server on the Internet. Similarly, communications from the Internet to the private network are received by the proxy server, analyzed, and forwarded appropriately. Since a proxy server operates at the application level, a separate proxy server may be required for each type of application. The proxy server authenticates each user, both from inside the private network as well as from the Internet. A strong authentication scheme is required to prevent unauthorized users from getting in or out of the private network.

The *SOCKS* server, which will be discussed in detail later in this chapter, also provides the gateway support through the firewall. A primary difference between the proxy server and the SOCKS server is that proxy requires a change in the way users access the Internet server, without modifying the client software. SOCKS, on the other hand, requires modifications to the client software, but no change is required to the user procedures.

Firewalls may also include a domain name service and a mail handling component. The *domain name service* isolates the name service of the private network from that of the Internet. As a result, the internal IP addresses of the private network hosts are not exposed to the Internet users. The *mail handling capability* ensures that any e-mail exchange between the private network and the Internet is processed through the firewall.

Grades of Firewall Security

Depending on its components, several grades of firewall security can be obtained. As shown in Figure 4.4, there is *no security* by allowing unrestricted open access between the Internet and the private network. Next, filters can be added to obtain a certain level of interception of unauthorized traffic. Next, the firewall can include the filters and the application gateways. A variety of proxy servers can be added along with different strengths of the authentication schemes. We can also improve the security for the private network by adding mail handling and name service functions to the firewall. Next, the firewall can reside on a secure operating system, thereby improving the underlying security for the firewall data and files. A firewall can also provide data confidentiality and integrity by implementing IP Security (described in Chapter 3). Finally, the company can deny any access to the Internet, thereby ensuring complete security (no access, no risks). Although this is seemingly a theoretical option, for certain highly secure environments, this may be the only prudent approach.

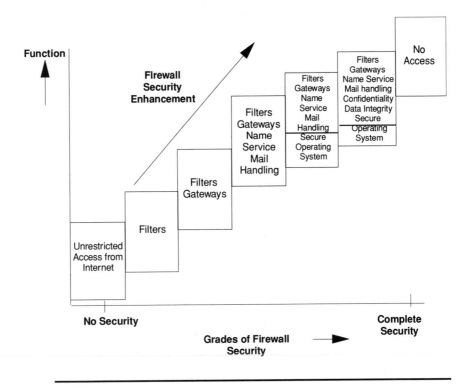

Figure 4.4: Grades of Security Provided by Firewall

Risks Not Addressed By Firewalls

There are certain types of security exposures to private networks that a firewall cannot address:

1. **Insider's Intrusion**: The firewall cannot protect the resources from attack by an internal user of the private network. The firewall is a gateway that simply intercepts the traffic between a private network and the Internet. As such, an insider may steal critical

company information or damage its resources without any awareness at the firewall. This threat can be addressed by implementing appropriate authentication and access control mechanisms, described earlier. Additionally, a department-level firewall can reduce the risk by intercepting traffic among different parts of a company (see Figure 4.2).

2. **Direct Internet Traffic**: A firewall is useful only if all the Internet traffic is handled through the firewall. The firewall cannot protect the resources of the private network from the traffic that takes place directly with the Internet bypassing the firewall. For example, if a user on the private network exchanges data over a direct access (such as a dial connection) to the Internet, then the firewall cannot intercept and examine that data. As such, it is critical for the private network to ensure that all the traffic to and from the Internet is transmitted through the firewall.

3. **Virus Protection**: Typically, a firewall cannot protect a private network from external viruses. A virus may be transferred to the private network using FTP or other means. To implement such protection, the firewall must implement the logic to detect viruses from the data stream.

Packet Filters

There are many router products in the industry that route IP packets based on the destination address in the IP header. If the router knows how to send the packet to the destination address, it does so. If the router does not know how to send the packet for the given destination address, it returns the packet using an ICMP *destination unreachable* message to the source address.

The routers that are used in firewalls are called *screening routers* or *filters*. Upon receiving a packet, a filter determines whether the packet should be discarded or forwarded to the destination address. This decision is based on the filter rules that are specified by the firewall administrator.

Filter Rules

Filter rules should be designed to reflect the company's security policy. The security policy determines the types of users and traffic that should be permitted to enter or to leave the private network.

Filter rules are often defined at the firewall installation time, although the rules can be modified, added, or deleted later. A filter rule consists of two parts: the action field and the selection criteria. The action field specifies the action to be taken if the packet is selected by this rule. Two types of actions are allowed:

1. **BLOCK (or DENY)**: implies that the selected packet should be rejected

2. **PERMIT (or ALLOW)**: specifies that the selected packet should be forwarded

The selection criteria can be based on a variety of parameters. Some of the common parameters are listed next.

1. **Source and Destination Address**: The filter rule includes an address mask for selecting a packet based on its source address and destination address.

The address selection is accomplished by specifying two dotted-decimal addresses. (See Table A.1 for IP address format). The first address is the desired address, and the second is a mask to select the bits in the address field. For example, suppose we want to select any packet with a source address that begins with 157.4.5. Then we will have 157.4.5.0 as the defined source address, and 255.255.255.0 as the address mask for selecting a packet. So for this address mask, the first three bytes of the mask will select all of the 24 bits of the first three bytes of a packet's source address. Next, the selected 24 bits are compared against 157.4.5. If there is a match, the packet is selected. A similar process can be used for the destination address.

2. **Source and Destination Port**: The filter rule may apply to a specific port number of the source host or the destination host.

3. **Protocol**: A packet also may be selected based on the higher level protocol. For example, a packet may be selected if it is using TCP, UDP, or ICMP protocols.

4. **Direction**: The packet can also be selected based on the direction of packet transmission with respect to the firewall. For example, an *inbound* packet is one coming from the Internet to the private network, and an *outbound* packet is one going in the opposite direction.

The last rule specifies to discard (block/reject) all packets, as described next.

The filter component of firewall works as follows. When a packet arrives at the filter component, it is tested against the first filter rule. If the first rule applies to the packet, then the specified action for that rule is carried out (the packet is rejected or forwarded). If this rule does not apply, then the second rule is checked, and so on. Note that at every rule, if the packet satisfies the selection criteria, then the action specified by that rule is performed and the filter processing is completed. Suppose the packet is not selected by any of the rules, up to the last one. The last rule, however, specifies to discard all packets. So, the last rule takes effect, and the packet is rejected. In short, the default action for packet filtering is to discard the packet, unless otherwise selected by a filter rule. This is a recommended security policy to prevent unauthorized packets to get into the private network. This process is shown in Figure 4.5.

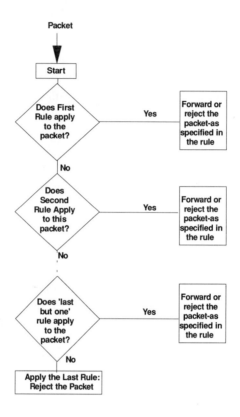

Figure 4.5: Processing a Packet through a Firewall Filter

Configuring Filters

A common concern pertaining to packet filtering relates to the complexity of configuring filter rules. The filter rules also require understanding of the TCP/IP addressing scheme. As a result, administrators may commit mistakes in defining the filter rules. The industry direction is to make it more simple to specify the rules and not require intricate knowledge of TCP/

IP. In addition, some utilities may be provided to check the syntax of the rules.

Source Address Spoofing Attack

The 1995 Source Address Spoofing Attack was described in Chapter 1. As stated, this attack was reported in January 1995 and impacted at least 50 hosts. Here, the attacker exploited the weakness that the source address of a packet can be changed. A firewall can be configured to resist such attacks as follows.

1. This attack exploits the weaknesses that the source address in the IP header is not secured. As such, a host can change the source address of a packet to appear as if it is coming from another host. To prevent such an attack, the filter rules should discard any packet from the Internet that contains the source address of a host inside the private network. The reason is that a packet from the Internet with the source address of a host inside a private network implies that the packet is fraudulent. As such, the filter rules should specify to discard the packet.

2. Suppose the administrator has detected that a certain host on the Internet is sending fraudulent packets by spoofing the source address. The system administrator can, in real time, add a new rule to discard any packets arriving from a host with that particular source address. Similarly, if a given target host is under attack, then the new filter rule can discard any packet destined for that destination address. The new rule should be added at the beginning of all the existing rules, thereby avoiding any impact to other traffic.

Proxy Server

Proxy Servers intercept and examine traffic at the TCP/IP application layer. A user on the private network is required to first access a proxy server before accessing an application server on the Internet. Similarly, a user on the Internet first accesses a proxy server before she or he is permitted to access a host on the private network. Most firewall proxy servers include TELNET and FTP. Since this service is at the application layer, separate proxy servers may be required for each type of application. The proxy client, however, can be implemented in several ways, as described later.

The purpose of a proxy server is to intercept the user access to an Internet application, authenticate the user, ensure that the user is authorized to access the application, and then permit the user to access the server on the Internet. A firewall may also provide the corresponding service for a user from the Internet to access an application server on the private network.

Figure 4.6 depicts the concept of a TELNET client and server using a proxy server. It shows that a TELNET client A is residing in the private network. The TELNET client A accesses the proxy server at the firewall for TELNET logon. Once the user at the TELNET client is authenticated by the proxy server, the proxy server verifies if the user can access TELNET over the Internet. If so, then the user is permitted to send a TELNET request on the Internet. A procedure for using the proxy server is described next.

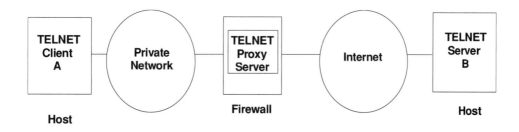

Figure 4.6: Firewall Proxy Gateway Example - TELNET

1. Client A on the private network sends a TELNET request to the firewall. (This is a new procedure for the user to follow, but requires no modifications to the client software.)

2. The proxy server at the firewall prompts the user to enter the user ID and a password.

3. The user enters the ID and the password. The proxy server authenticates the user by verifying the password for the userID. If user authentication fails, the user request is rejected. If user authentication succeeds, proceed to step 4.

4. The user sends a TELNET request to TELNET server B on a host over the Internet.

5. Server B authenticates the user. If the user is successfully authenticated, proceed to step 6; otherwise the request is rejected.

6. For any message going from client A to server B, the firewall code intercepts the traffic and replaces the source address of the IP packet with that of the firewall's address. As such, the internal addresses of the host on the private network are not exposed to the hosts on the Internet.

Finally, there may be files such as a standards document, that are made available through anonymous FTP support. In effect, Internet users can access these files directly without requiring any authentication. To support that, some private networks provide a server outside the firewall. Such an externalized server restricts Internet user access to only the local resources residing at the server. Clearly, the connection from the external-ized server to the private network should be through the fire-wall, as shown in Figure 4.7.

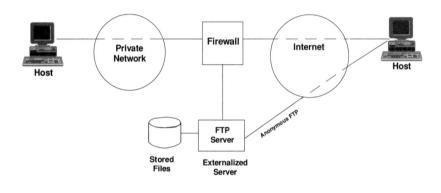

Figure 4.7: Externalized FTP Server

Approaches for Proxy Server

As described, a proxy system consists of a proxy server at the firewall. For the client side, there are three approaches to implement proxy.

1. **Customize User Procedure**: In this approach, the user procedures are modified to implement the proxy. The preceding discussion of proxy server is based on this concept. An important benefit for this

scheme is that it requires no impact to the client software. Given the extensive presence of existing TCP/IP client software, this approach is quite attractive for implementing access to the Internet.

The drawback of this scheme is that the user has to be trained for an extra step to logon the proxy server. For large sites that have been using the TCP/IP applications for a long time, the user training may be a time-consuming and expensive process.

2. **Customize Client Software**: This approach requires modifications to the client software and provides transparency to users in accessing the Internet. This transparency is attained by implementing additional software at the client and the firewall that intercepts and directs the application traffic. A common implementation of such an approach is called SOCKS. SOCKS was mentioned earlier and is described later in detail.

3. Another approach is to contain all the software modifications for proxy support in the firewall. In this case, neither the client software nor the user procedures require any changes.This approach still requires that all the messages to and from the Internet are transmitted through the firewall. Typically, a user sends a request to connect to a server on the Internet. Transparent to the user, the firewall intercepts the request, authenticates the user, verifies the request, and proceeds with the connection appropriately.

SOCKS

SOCKS provides a customized client approach for providing proxy services. In effect, SOCKS requires modifications to the client software to accommodate the interception at the firewall between the user on the private network and the server on the Internet. Typically, SOCKS is used for access from hosts on a private network to the Internet servers.

SOCKS protocol was published by David Koblas and Michelle R. Koblas (Koblas 1992). SOCKS protocol Version 4 is described in Leech (1994). SOCKS is also described in some of the security books such as Chapman (1995) and IBMFW (1995).

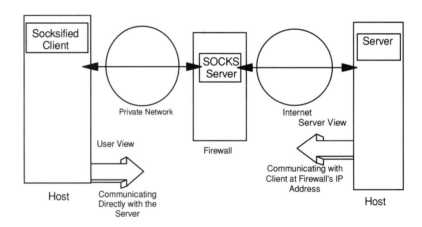

Figure 4.8: SOCKS Support in Firewalls

Figure 4.8 depicts a typical SOCKS implementation. SOCKS requires modifications to TCP/IP clients to accommodate interactions with the SOCKS server. A TCP/IP client that has been modified to handle SOCKS interactions is called a *socksi-*

fied client. A socksified client issues SOCKS calls transparent to the user. The SOCKS server resides at the firewall and interacts with the socksified clients. There are no changes required for the server residing at the Internet.

SOCKS Version 4 (Leech 1994) works as follows. The goal for SOCKS is to provide a general framework for TCP/IP applications to securely use the services of a firewall. The protocol is independent of the supported TCP/IP application. When a TCP/IP client requires access to a server, then the client code must first open a TCP/IP connection to the SOCKS server. The conventional port number for SOCKS service is 1080. If the connection request is accepted, then the client sends a request to the SOCKS server. The request includes the following information:

- Desired destination port
- Desired destination address
- Authentication information

The SOCKS server evaluates the information in the request. It either accepts the request and establishes the connection to the Internet server, or denies the request. This evaluation depends on the configuration data of the SOCKS server. In either case, the SOCKS server sends a reply to the client. The reply includes information indicating whether the request was successful.

A clear advantage of the SOCKS protocol is that it is transparent to the user. The user accesses the Internet without requiring any awareness of the intervening firewall. As such, there is no user training required when a firewall is installed for the private network. However, this approach requires changes to the client software. As a result, an upgrade is required for the user workstations. This upgrade can be provided either at the application level or at the underlying TCP/IP code. In the former case, each application client, such as TELNET and FTP, must be socksified. Alternatively, the SOCKS protocol can be implemented in the underlying TCP/IP stack so that it is transparent to the TCP/IP applications. As such, each TCP/IP application can make transparent use of the SOCKS services.

Finally, it should be noted that any gateway approach relies heavily on the underlying authentication scheme. A weak authentication scheme can easily defeat the purpose for the firewall. This topic is addressed next.

User Authentication

A typical TCP/IP application, such as TELNET, requires the entry of a userID and password for authentication. However, unless otherwise protected, the password is transmitted in the clear over the Internet. The primary concern here is the protection of passwords over the Internet. We consider this issue in the context of authenticating the user and the administrator.

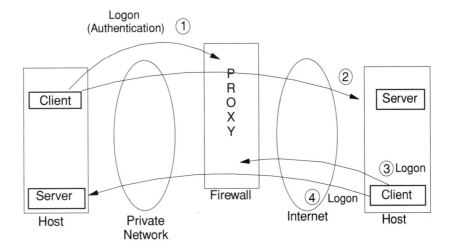

Figure 4.9: Authentification Using Firewall as the Gateway

Private Network to Internet

Consider the two scenarios for user authentication shown in
Figure 4.9. The first scenario consists of steps 1 and 2. In this
scenario, the client begins by sending the userID and the password to the firewall. This exchange takes place over the secure
private network. The security exposure for a password theft is
arguably less in this scenario compared to the password trans-
missions over the Internet. Next, the user logs on the Internet
host by sending the ID and password over the Internet. The

topic of password transmission over the Internet is included in the next scenario.

Internet to Private Network

In the second scenario, the user logs from the Internet to a server on the private network. This is shown as steps 3 and 4 in Figure 4.9. First, the user sends an ID and a password to the firewall. However, even an encrypted password can be copied over the Internet. This may lead to a replay attack, where the intruder enters the (stolen) encrypted password and gains access to the firewall and then to the private network. To thwart such an attack, it is desirable to use one-time passwords. Token cards are available that generate random passwords to be used only once, as described in Chapter 2. In this case, even if the password is stolen, it is of no use to the intruder, since a one-time password may not be accepted after its first use.

Authenticating the Administrator

Consider the process for a user to log on a firewall as an administrator. In late 1994, I heard of an unconfirmed story that an intruder got into a firewall as an administrator from the Internet. The intruder attempted various passwords over the Internet, and at last succeeded in guessing the correct password.

Assuming the firewall is residing on a UNIX system, there are two precautions to address such an attack.

1. The administrator should always be required to use a one-time password for gaining remote access to the firewall.

2. The (firewall) administrator logon should not be accepted from the Internet side. In effect, the administrator logon to the firewall is permitted only from the private network. This precaution can greatly reduce the chances of a hacker gaining administrator access to the firewall from the Internet.

Finally, the password storage files are a well-known target of attacks by hackers. The topic of securely storing passwords is addressed in Ahuja (1996).

Domain Name System

A *domain name system* provides the name to address translation in a TCP/IP network. A firewall can provide a modified name-server function for users residing inside and outside the private network. However, the firewall should not divulge the IP addresses of hosts inside the private network. So for inquiries from hosts on the Internet, the firewall should resolve all the names of hosts inside the private network to the IP address of the firewall. For inquiries from hosts inside the private network, the firewall forwards name-to-address resolution for hosts on the Internet.

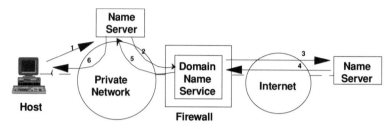

a. Name / Address Resolution Request from a Host on the Private Network for an Internet Host

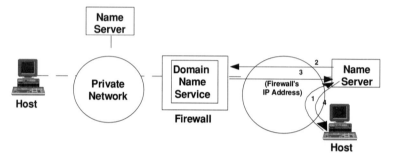

b. Name / Address Resolution Request from a Host on the Internet for a Host on the Private Network

Figure 4.10: Domain Name Service in Firewall

Figure 4.10 shows two sequences for name-address resolution. First, a client from the private network requests a name-address resolution for a host residing on the Internet. The name server on the private network forwards this request to the firewall, as shown in Figure 4.10a. The domain name service at the firewall accesses the name server on the Internet, obtains the IP address of the requested host name, and sends this IP address to the name server on the private network. The name server on the private network forwards this response to the client that originated the request.

Next, assume that a client on the Internet requests the IP address of a host located inside the private network. The request goes to a name server on the Internet, and the name server forwards it to the firewall. The firewall responds with its own IP address, as shown in Figure 4.10b. As such, hosts on the Internet are aware of only the firewall's IP address for hosts residing inside the private network.

Dynamic Address Allocation

A firewall can provide a feature so that the private network can assign its own IP addresses. These addresses can be allocated without regard to the Internet addresses. Whenever a packet is to be assigned an Internet address, the firewall can choose an address from a pool of addresses allocated by the Internet. As such, the firewall can provide address allocation and translation in such a way that the private network addresses need not be the same as those available from the Internet.

There are two distinct benefits of this approach. First, consider a company that has been using its own private IP addresses. For such a company, it will not require any changes to the addresses to connect to the Internet. It may also reduce the number of IP addresses to be assigned to the company by the Internet. Note that some of the IP address classes are running out of available addresses. Secondly, the company's internal IP addresses are not divulged to the external Internet users. This provides additional security by making it difficult for an intruder to find the internal IP addresses.

Mail Handling

E-*mail* (electronic mail) is one of the primary reasons for private networks to connect to the Internet. It is extensively used by Internet users to exchange information with each other. Typically, *Simple Mail Transfer Protocol (SMTP)* is used to handle mail on the Internet, although secure e-mail schemes have been developed and implemented (see Chapter 3).

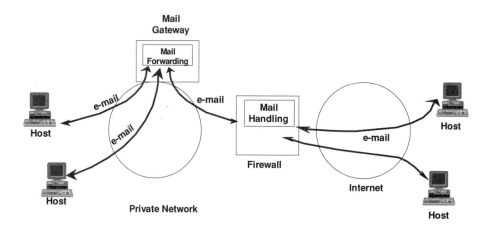

Figure 4.11: Mail Handling at the Firewall

E-mail may also need to be intercepted and forwarded appropriately. The deamon (background program running in a server) for e-mail, *SENDMAIL*, has been known to be exposed to several vulnerabilities and continues to be the target of attacks.

To protect the private network, one approach is to provide a mail gateway on the private network, as shown in Figure 4.11. E-mail originating from the private network is first sent to the mail gateway. The mail gateway, in turn, selects the e-mail destined for the Internet and forwards it to the firewall mail handling program. For the e-mail received from the Internet, the firewall forwards it to the mail gateway on the private network. To the Internet users, the firewall is the only exposed mail gateway. There are some benefits to such an approach:

1. Each e-mail message from the Internet is received by the firewall and not by the mail gateway of the private network. This is desirable, since the firewall is better equipped to handle any intrusion attempts than a mail gateway (another host) on the private network.

2. There is a single point of control of all the e-mail between the private network and the Internet. In this way, a site can implement controls to intercept and check for any viruses or other malicious software being transmitted to the private network. The mail gateway can also verify that only authorized users are permitted to send or receive mail over the Internet.

IP Security

The topic of IP Security was presented in Chapter 3. Firewalls are the first products that are implementing the IP Security standards, although the standard also applies to the workstation operating systems.

User Certification

5

To accomplish secure commerce on the Internet, there must be a mechanism for individuals to verify their identity and digitally sign the purchase or sale order. *User certification* relates to validating the identity claimed by individuals over a public network. Consider a hypothetical sale of shares of stock shown in Figure 5.1. The customer, say Tom, sends a request to his stockbroker to sell 500 shares. The broker receives the request and sells the shares.

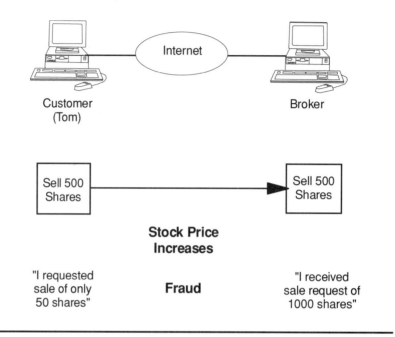

Figure 5.1: Hypothetical Example for nonrepudiation

Tom and the broker each may have a concern with the transaction.

- How can the broker establish that it was indeed Tom who issued the sale order? Furthermore, the broker must possess the proof to establish that Tom ordered the sale of exactly 500 shares, no more and no less.

- How can Tom establish that the broker received the order to sell exactly 500 shares, as Tom had requested? Tom must possess the proof to establish that he ordered the sale of exactly 500 shares.

Note that even if the transaction was encrypted using a shared key, the broker and Tom would still not have a way to trust each other's actions. This is because Tom or the broker can modify the transaction using the shared key. Such a dispute can be resolved only by instituting a mechanism that would protect the seller and the buyer from each other. The mechanism should be capable of establishing that Tom indeed ordered the sale of exactly 500 shares, and the broker cannot modify the sale order. This mechanism is called *nonrepudiation*.

In the traditional world, the answer is straightforward—we can require Tom to sign the request in front of a notary public or fill out and sign an appropriate form. However, while transacting business over the Internet, there is no face-to-face meeting or direct involvement of a notary public.

User Validation

We will review some of the alternatives that will lead to the conclusion that nonrepudiation can be addressed primarily through a public key scheme described later.

1. The first alternative could be for the user to authenticate by entering the password, as described in Chapter 2. Such an approach is sufficient for a system to verify the identity of a user to the application. However, this verification is valid only at the time of session start-up or logon. A password entry by a user at logon does not guarantee the integrity of the data contents of a request during a session. So, a password is useful to initiate a session but does not protect the contents of a request during the session.

2. The next alternative may be to consider the encryption schemes. The encryption schemes, such as those
described in Chapter 2, use an encryption key that is
shared between the sender and the receiver. The
sender uses the key to encrypt the data, and the
receiver uses it to decrypt the encrypted data. As
such, the data has been protected from unauthorized
modifications during transmission. However, it does
not protect the sender and receiver from each other.

For the example shown in Figure 5.1, consider the use of
encryption schemes described in Chapter 2. Tom encrypts the
sale request using the encryption key. The broker uses the same
key to decrypt the request and sells the shares. Now consider
the fraud when the broker modifies the request to show that
Tom had requested to sell 1000 shares (since, let us say, the
share prices have gone up). Since the broker possesses the
encryption key, he or she can modify Tom's sale request. Similarly, Tom could falsely say that he had asked for the sale of
5000 shares. As such, both Tom and the broker can change the
contents of the request, and neither of them has a recourse to
prove the actual contents of the original request.

3. Finally, we come to the point. To establish that the
sender indeed sent a certain request, the sender
should encrypt the request with a unique key that is
known only to the sender. The receiver should have a
different key that should permit the receiver to
decrypt the encrypted request. Now the sender and
receiver can save the request to establish the original
contents of the request. Such a scheme would clearly
require that the encryption key must be different than
the decryption key. An encryption scheme that
requires different keys for encryption and decryption
is called an *Asymmetric Encryption* scheme.

Asymmetric Encryption

If a cryptographic scheme uses the same key for encryption as well as decryption, it is called *symmetric encryption*. Examples of symmetric encryption schemes include DES, CDMF, and IDEA, described in Chapter 2.

If the encryption key cannot be the same as the decryption key, it is called *asymmetric encryption*. An example of asymmetric encryption is the public key cryptology.

Public Key Cryptology

In 1976, Diffie and Hellman published a remarkable breakthrough in cryptology (Diffie 1976). They were concerned with the need for secure distribution of secret encryption keys. For symmetric encryption schemes, there is a need for the sender and the receiver to have access to the same encryption key. Although the data can be securely transmitted after encryption, it is harder to distribute the encryption key securely. Diffie and Hellman have addressed this concern in their paper.

Public key cryptosystems rely on the use of one key for encryption and a related but different key for decryption. Furthermore, it is computationally infeasible to obtain a decryption key with only the knowledge of the encryption key and the cryptographic algorithm, as described in Stallings (1995).

Rivest, Shamir, and Adleman developed a *public-key cryptosystem*, as described in Rivest (1978). This algorithm is also called RSA, where the three letters reflect the initials of the three authors. In the RSA algorithm, either of the two keys can be used for encryption, while the other key is used for decryption.

Every user is assigned two keys;

- a *private key* that is known only to the user
- a *public key* that is known to everyone

The process of encryption and decryption takes place as shown in Figure 5.2.

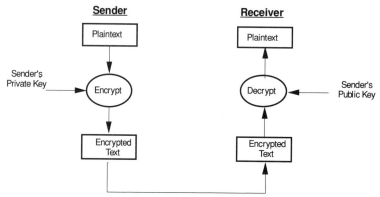

Figure 5.2(i): Authentication But No Confidentiality

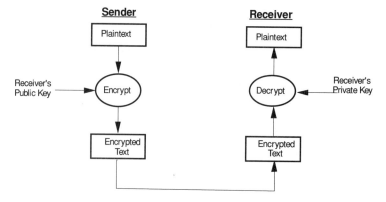

Figure 5.2(ii): Confidentiality But No Authentication

Figure 5.2: Public Key Usage

Each user has a key pair. So, the sender and the receiver each have a public key and a private key. In Figure 5.2(i), the sender uses his or her private key to encrypt the plaintext. The receiver uses the sender's public key to decrypt the encrypted text. Since only the sender knows his or her private key, the receiver is assured that the encrypted text originated from the sender who owns that particular public/private key pair. However, the encrypted text can be decrypted by any user, since everyone has access to the sender's public key. Although the sender's authentication is achieved, this transmission did not ensure the confidentiality of the data. The reason is that anyone can decrypt the encrypted text using the commonly available public key of the sender.

Now consider the scheme depicted in Figure 5.2(ii). Here, the sender encrypts the plaintext using the receiver's public key. The receiver decrypts the encrypted data by using his or her private key. Since only the receiver knows his or her private key, no other person can decrypt the encrypted text. However, anyone can send this encrypted message using the commonly available public key of the receiver. In this approach, we achieved confidentiality but no authentication.

These two approaches can be combined to achieve authentication and confidentiality. In the combined approach, the sender encrypts the message with the sender's private key to provide authentication of the source. The resulting ciphertext is encrypted again using the receiver's public key to provide confidentiality. The receiver first decrypts the message using the receiver's private key and then decrypts the resulting text using the sender's public key.

RSA Public Key Algorithm

As stated, the RSA public algorithm describes a scheme where the public/private key pair is used to encrypt and decrypt the message. Let P be the plaintext block with a binary value less than some number n. Then the encrypted block C is computed as follows:

$$C = P^e \bmod n,$$
$$\text{and } P = C^d \bmod n,$$
$$= (P^e)^d \bmod n.$$
$$= P^{ed} \bmod n.$$

The public key of the receiver is (e, n) and the private key is (d, n). The sender has access to the receiver's public key (e, n) and uses e to encrypt the plaintext using the expression $C = P^e \bmod n$.

The receiver knows its private key (d, n) and uses d to decrypt the block using the expression $P = C^d \bmod n$. The number n is known to the receiver and the sender as part of the public/private keys. The mathematical details of the algorithm can be found in Schneier (1994) and Stallings (1995).

Digital Signature

We described the concept of encryption and message digest in Chapter 2. A *message digest* is obtained by applying a one-way hash function to the message. This digest is often appended to the message. The receiver can apply the same one-way hash function to the message. If the result matches with the received digest, then the receiver assumes that the message was not tampered during transmission. The digest is computed using a secret key that should be known only to the sender and the receiver.

This scheme protects the sender and the receiver from an attack in which a third-party intercepts and modifies the message. However, it does not protect the sender and receiver from each other. For example, the receiver could modify the message, recompute the digest, and claim that it came from the sender. To protect the sender and receiver from each other, we can use a public-key scheme as follows.

Upon computing the digest of the message, the digest is encrypted using the sender's private key. The receiver verifies the digest by decrypting it using the sender's public key. The important point here is that the receiver can establish that a given message was indeed sent by the sender by showing the received ciphertext, including the digest that was encrypted by the sender's private key. This is because only the sender is expected to have his or her private key. Thus, this scheme provides *nonrepudiation* between two parties.

User Certification

In the public-key scheme, the sender's public key is made available to each potential receiver. A receiver needs the sender's public key in order to decrypt the encrypted text from the sender. Additionally, the sender must be capable of assuring the receiver that a given public key is indeed from the sender.

We need to address two problems:

1. Provide the sender's public key to the receiver.

2. Include information to establish the identity of the sender whose public key is being provided to the receiver.

Consider an example. Sally wants to send some encrypted text to Dave, so she encrypts the data using her private key and sends the ciphertext to Dave. Dave uses Sally's public key to decrypt the message. But how is Dave assured that the public key actually belongs to Sally? In other words, it could be an imposter with a a different public key claiming that it is from Sally.

This problem can be solved in the same way we use IDs or badges. A driver's license links the license number with the owner's picture and date of birth. As a result, we can associate the driver's license with a person through the picture on the license. A similar approach is used to establish a sender's identity in digital certificates.

A *digital certificate* or *digital ID* simply links an RSA public key with certain identifications of its owner. For example, my digital certificate could link my name and address to a particular public key. But my digital certificate must be attested (or signed) by a recognized authority. So, for you to accept my digital certificate, the certificate must be signed by someone (e.g., a notary public) that you would trust.

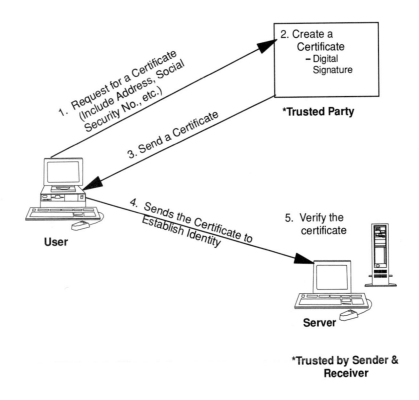

1. Request for a Certificate (Include Address, Social Security No., etc.)

2. Create a Certificate
   – Digital Signature

*Trusted Party

3. Send a Certificate

4. Sends the Certificate to Establish Identity

User

5. Verify the certificate

Server

*Trusted by Sender & Receiver

Figure 5.3: Creation and Use of Digital Certificate

Figure 5.3 depicts how trust is established using digital certificates; we discuss it through an example. Sue needs to communicate with Bill, so she needs to provide Bill with her public
key. In addition Sue must prove that this public key really
belongs to her. So, Sue requests a certificate from a trusted
party. This trusted party is accepted as a reliable authority to
issue certificates. Before the trusted party issues a certificate to
Sue, it asks her to provide certain identification information. If
the identification information is accepted by the trusted party,
then it creates a certificate. Next, the trusted party computes a

one-way hash function on the information, and encrypts it using its private key. Now Sue sends the certificate to Bill. Bill already possesses the trusted party's public key, and uses this public key to decrypt the digest and verify that the certificate was indeed sent and signed by the particular trusted party. As a result, Bill accepts that the public key in the certificate belongs to Sue.

X.509 Certificates

X.509 certificates define the commonly used form of digital certificates. CCITT Recommendation X.509 is part of CCITT's X.500 series of recommendations. X.500 specifies the directory service; X.509 describes the authentication service using X.500 directory.

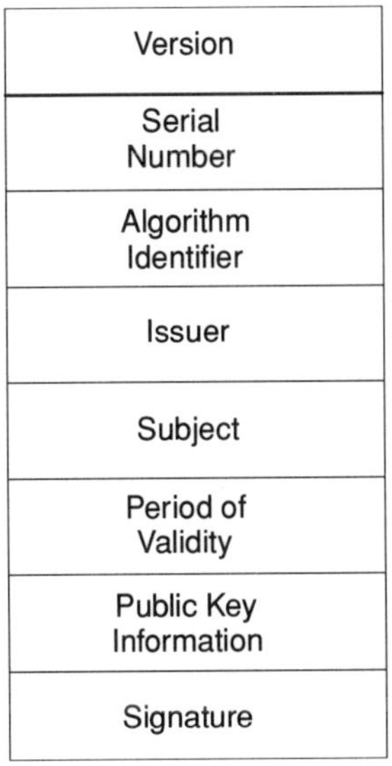

Version
Serial Number
Algorithm Identifier
Issuer
Subject
Period of Validity
Public Key Information
Signature

Figure 5.4: X.509 Certificate

Figure 5.4 depicts the general format of an X.509 certificate.

Version: The version of the certificate format. X.509 Versions 1, 2, and 3 are defined.

Serial Number: The number assigned by the *Certificate Authority (CA)* to the user. This number is unique within all the certificates issued by the CA.

Algorithm Identifier: The algorithm used for the digital signature of the certificate.

Issuer: The certificate authority (CA) that issued and signed this certificate.

Period of Validity: Two dates: the certificate is not valid before the first date or after the second date.

Subject: The name and other identifiers of the user for whom this certificate is issued. For example, this may include user name and address.

Public Key Information: The user's public key and the algorithms for which this key should be used.

Signature: The issuer (CA) applies a one-way hash function on all of the fields except this signature field. The result is encrypted using the CA's private key. When someone receives this certificate, the receiver applies the CA's public key to decrypt the signature. A successful decryption and integrity check assures the receiver that the certificate was indeed issued by the specified CA.

Certificate Revocation

To prevent fraud and mischief, a certificate revocation mechanism is designed. Before expiration, a certificate may be revoked for one of the following reasons:

- The user's private key is assumed to be compromised.

- The user is no longer certified by this CA.

- The CA's private key is assumed to be compromised.

Each CA maintains a list of all those certificates that are revoked but not expired. This list is called *Certificate Revocation List (CRL)*. Whenever a user receives a certificate, it must check whether the certificate has been revoked. As such, a CRL is maintained by each user and CA. The CA must provide updates to its users of any changes to the CRL.

Certificate Distribution

Figure 5.3 depicts the scheme to generate and distribute X.509 certificates. It works as follows. A user wishes to prove his or her identity to a server. Assuming that the user has not yet obtained a certificate, the following steps are executed.

1. The user requests a digital certificate that he or she can send to a server to prove his or her identity.

2. The CA creates a digital certificate. The CA applies a one-way hash function (specifies it in the certificate) on the certificate and obtains the message digest. Next, the CA encrypts this digest using the CA's private key and appends the encrypted digest to the certificate.

3. The CA sends the entire data unit to the user.

4. The user sends this certificate to the server. In addition, the user saves this certificate to send to other servers in the future.

5. The server receives the certificate. It reads the name of the CA from the certificate. Then, the server retrieves the public key of this particular CA and decrypts the encrypted message digest. Now the server applies the one-way hash function specified in the certificate and used by the CA. It compares its result with the decrypted message digest. If the results match, then the server checks the validity of the certificate by using the period-of-validity field. Finally, the CA checks whether the certificate is listed

in CRL (described earlier). If this certificate passes all these checks, then the server is assured of the authenticity of the user. For the above scheme to work, each server should have access to the public keys of major certificate authorities.

Finally, this description applies to a user requiring a certificate from a CA. Each server will also need to authenticate itself to its clients. As such, the servers also need a certificate from the CA. To obtain a certificate, the server executes a scenario similar to that used by the client.

Certificate Chains and Hierarchies

Certificates will be issued by several organizations for different purposes. A company may issue certificates to its employees, a university may issue certificates to its students, or a city may issue certificates to its citizens. The certificate (information) may be stored as encoded data on various IDs and badges. The criteria to issue certificates may also vary with different certificate authorities. Some CAs may issue a certificate based on the name and address; others may require proof of date of birth, or fingerprints, and so on. Finally, some institutions such as courts may accept only notarized certificates.

It is conceivable that there will be more than one CA involved in issuing certificates. It is also likely that a user may possess more than one certificate, just as we carry more than one proof of identity today such as credit cards and a driver's licence.

Consider a chain of certificates. The postal department of a country may authorize various companies to issue certificates to their employees. Each company may issue certificates to its regional offices. Each regional office in turn may issue certificates to its branch offices, and branch offices may issue certificates to their employees. At every step, the appropriate CA digitally signs the certificate, as shown in Figure 5.5. So when an employee of this company sends his or her certificate, it would include digital signatures of three CAs. The receiver of such a certificate can verify the certificate by using the public keys of the three CAs in the chain.

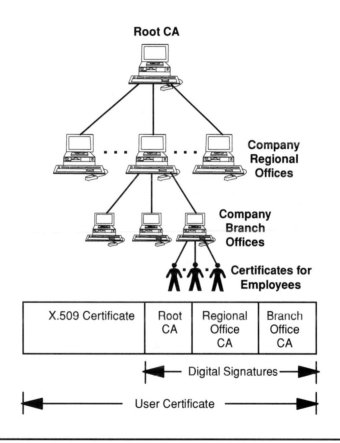

Figure 5.5: Certificate Chains

To make this scheme work, a CA must sufficiently publicize its public key. This is important so as to prevent distribution and proliferation of forged certificates. For example, a fake company can distribute its public key under the name of a well-known CA and then issue bogus certificates.

Finally, it is critical that the CA's private key must be securely guarded. A loss of a CA's private key can lead to fraudulent certificates and signatures.

Certificate Usage

X.509 certificates will become the backbone for secure commerce on the Internet. X.509 digital certificates are supported in many network security technologies. Examples include PEM (Privacy Enhanced Mail), PGP (Pretty Good Privacy), Secure Socket Layer (SSL), Secure HyperText Transfer Protocol (S-HTTP), and Secure Electronic Transaction (SET). We described PEM and PGP in Chapter 3; we will describe their use of X.509 certificates next. S-HTTP, SSL, and SET will be described in later chapters along with their use of X.509 certificates.

X.509 Certificates for PEM

PEM uses the X.509 certificates for establishing the identity of the sender to the receiver. PEM uses a certificate hierarchy proposed by the PEM standard. It starts with IPRA (Internet Policy Registration Authority) as the highest level of CA hierarchy. Conceptually, IPRA will issue certificates to PCA (Policy Certification Authorities). PCAs will issue certificates to CAs, and CAs in turn will issue certificates to users.

Prior to sending an encrypted message using PEM, the sender must receive a certificate for each recipient and must validate these certificates. The sender validates the certificates by decrypting the digital signature in the certificate, and uses the public key (supplied separately) of the certificate issuer to decrypt each digital signature. If the certificate is issued by a CA hierarchy, then each step of the chain is validated.

Next, the public key of each recipient's certificate is extracted and used to encrypt the *data encryption key* (DEK). The DEK is used to encrypt the message itself. The encrypted DEK is inserted in a field in the message header.

Upon receipt of the message, the receiver extracts the encrypted DEK field. Next, the receiver uses its private key to decrypt the encrypted DEK. Now the receiver uses the DEK to decrypt the message.

The X.509 certificates are used for message integrity and data origin authentication as follows. The originator computes a *message integrity code (MIC)*, encrypts the MIC using its private key, and includes the result in the message header. The recipient first validates the originator's certificate by using the public key of the issuer and by verifying whether the certificate has been revoked. Next, it extracts the public key from the originator's certificate and uses it to decrypt the MIC. Finally, the receiver computes the MIC and compares it to the MIC value decrypted from the received message to verify the integrity and data origin authentication.

Details on use of X.509 certificates in PEM can be found in RFC 1422 (Kent 1993a).

X.509 Certificates for PGP

The PGP approach for certificate usage relies on the notion that trust is a social concept. For example, although a bank needs complete verification before letting me withdraw a large sum of money, you do not need to verify my identity if I send you an unsolicited letter praising the beauties of the Himalayas.

PGP uses the concept of common trust among communicating parties. Whereas PEM uses the hierarchical trust model, PGP uses the notion that people trust their friends. If you and I have a common friend, then you will accept my identity if our common friend signs my certificate. It is possible that my certificate is signed by several of my friends, and if you trust one of them, you will probably accept my certificate.

The PGP approach makes it relatively easy for individuals to obtain signed certificates. For a hierarchical model, users must share a common hierarchy in order to communicate with each other. A drawback of the PGP approach is that you cannot verify the identity of every other user. In PGP, there may be several isolated user groups that share their trust within the group. In contrast, PEM uses a single hierarchy to issue certificates.

Key Escrow Encryption Systems

Key escrow pertains to storing and retrieving keys for providing backup decryption of the encrypted text. This topic has been discussed at great length over the last few years in the context of the Clipper chip (described later). A series of papers on this topic were published in the March 1996 issue of *Commu-nications of the ACM* (Denning 1996, Walker 1996, Maher 1996, Ganesan 1996).

A *key escrow* system refers to the safeguarding of the data recovery keys of an encryption system. The *data recovery keys* normally are not the encryption or the decryption key used in the system. The data recovery keys provide the means to determine the encryption and the decryption keys of the system. A *key escrow encryption system* is an encryption system that allows authorized parties to decrypt the ciphertext. An authorized party decrypts the ciphertext by accessing information from one or more trusted parties that hold data recovery keys for the encryption system.

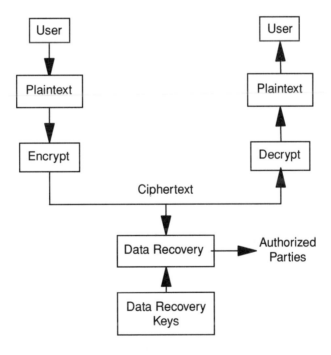

Figure 5.6: Key Escrow Systems

The basic components of a key escrow system are outlined in Figure 5.6. The encryption and decryption of data takes place as described earlier (see Figure 2.9). The data recovery is accomplished by providing the decryption capability to authorized parties.

Denning (1996) provides a detailed description of a model for key escrow encryption systems. The paper also tabulates characteristics of various key escrow systems.

Clipper

Clipper is an NSA-designed VLSI chip. According to Lynch (1996), the chip is designed for AT&T commercial secure voice products. Each chip includes the following information stored in a special on-chip memory:

- A serial number uniquely assigned to the chip
- A unit key that is unique to the chip
- A family key that is common to a family of chips
- Specialized control software

Each chip is uniquely programmed with this information before it is delivered to the customers. In addition, each chip has a special key that is not used for encryption or decryption; it is used to encrypt a copy of each user's message key. Thus, anyone in possession of this special key can decrypt any messages protected by this chip.

The intent of the scheme is that an authorized party can decrypt the wire-tapped information. According to Lynch (1996), the claim is that only the government will know this key, and they will use it only if authorized by the court. Furthermore, the key will be split in two parts and secured by two different agencies of the government. Each piece is completely useless without the other, according to Kaufman (1995).

There has been a controversy over the Clipper chip and the key escrow systems. Those in favor of the escrow systems view this as an approach to provide encryption to the public at large, while allowing the law enforcement agencies to monitor communications of illegal activities. Those opposed argue that it is an intrusion into the privacy of the citizens. For additional details, see Barlow (1993).

RSA and DES

RSA and DES may be used together to maximize security and performance. Although DES can be conveniently used for bulk data encryption, the DES keys cannot easily be transported in a secure way. A common approach is to encrypt the data using the DES key and transmit the DES key after encrypting it under the RSA key. In certain situations, if DES keys can be communicated through other secure means, RSA encryption may not be required. However, note that the RSA public key can also be used to provide the digital signature for nonrepudiation.

The public key cryptology and X.509 certificates are rapidly gaining acceptance on the Internet. Additional details on these topics can be found in Schneier (1994), Stallings (1995), Diffie (1976), Rivest (1978), Kent (1993a), Schneier (1995), and Ahuja (1996).

Web Security

The *World Wide Web*, or *Web*, provides a user-friendly interface for communications over the Internet. As described in detail in Appendix B, the Web relies on Hypertext Transfer Protocols (HTTP) to communicate over the TCP/IP network. The security components for TCP/IP and the Web are shown in Figure 3.1. In this chapter, we address the various security aspects of the Web.

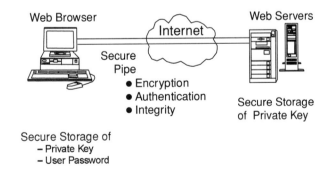

Figure 6.1: Web Security

A typical Web connection is shown in Figure 6.1. Security requirements for the Web include provision for a secure pipe between the **Web browser** and **Web server**. The Web browser is also called a **browser** or a **Web client**. Similar to e-mail, the Web is required to authenticate the data origin, provide encryption, and ensure integrity of data between the client and the server.

The security for a Web connection is provided in two parts: by safeguarding the security data for the Web connection, and by protecting the Web transactions.

Secure Storage

The browser and the server must protect any private data for security services. The browser needs to store securely the user password, the user's private key, and other related security data. One of the approaches to assure such security is to provide users with a pluggable token card. The private data is stored on the card and the user is expected to carry the card with him or her. While working on the Web, the user plugs in the card to the browser, as described later in Chapter 7.

Secure Web Transactions

For certain types of transactions, it may be necessary to protect the communications between the Web browser and the server. There are several approaches to protect Web transactions:

1. Secure Socket Layer (SSL)

2. Secure HyperText Transfer Protocol (S-HTTP)

3. Private Communication Technology (PCT)

4. Web Security through the use of Generic Security Service Application Program Interface (GSSAPI)

Each scheme allows negotiation of security mechanisms between the browser and the server prior to exchanging transactional data. Figure 6.2 depicts the protocol layers of TCP/IP relative to S-HTTP and SSL. As we describe next, SSL can support any application at the sockets level, but S-HTTP is specifically designed to secure HTTP.

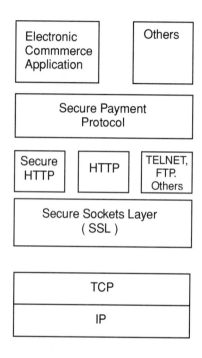

Figure 6.2: Hierarchical Layers of Web Security Protocols

Secure Sockets Layer (SSL)

Netscape developed a security protocol for communications between the Web browsers and servers. *Secure Sockets Layer (SSL)* provides privacy on the Internet. A description of SSL is available in Hickman (1995), an Internet draft dated June 1995. SSL is by far the most pervasive security protocol for Web connection.

SSL provides authentication, encryption, and message integrity. It is designed to authenticate the server, and optionally, the client. SSL uses TCP as the underlying transport protocol for reliable data transmission and reception. Since SSL resides at the socket level, it is independent of the higher-level application. As such, it can provide security services to higher-level protocols such as TELNET, FTP, and HTTP, as shown in Figure 6.2. This description of SSL is based on Wayner (1996) and Hickman (1995).

SSL consists of two protocols, SSL Record Protocol and SSL Handshake Protocol. The SSL Record Protocol is described later. The *SSL Handshake Protocol* is used to negotiate security parameters for an SSL connection.

SSL Handshake Protocol

In the *SSL Handshake Protocol*, the client and server exchange a series of messages to negotiate security enhancements. The SSL Handshake Protocol consists of six phases, described next.

The first phase is the *Hello* phase; it is used to agree upon a set of algorithms for privacy and authentication. In addition, this phase also discovers any existing session-ID from a previous session. The client begins by sending the *CLIENT-HELLO* message to the server. It includes three types of information: the type of encryption scheme that the client can handle, the session ID left over from a previous broken session (if any), and a random data to challenge the server. If the server recognizes the old session ID, then the session is restarted. If it is a new session, then the server sends an X.509 certificate to the client. The certificate includes the server's public key that is signed by the private key of a certificate authority (CA). The client will use the CA's public key to decipher the server's public key. The server's public key, in turn, is used to read the server's certificate. The following messages are exchanged in this phase:

CLIENT-HELLO
SERVER-HELLO

The second phase is the *Key Exchange* phase. In this phase, information on keys is exchanged between the client and the server. At the end of the phase, both sides have a shared *Master Key*. SSL Version 3 supports three key exchange algorithms: RSA, Diffie-Hellman, and Fortezza-KEA. The key is sent as encrypted text using the server's public key. The following messages are exchanged in this phase:

CLIENT-MASTER-KEY
CLIENT-DH-KEY

The third phase is the *Session Key Production* phase; it provides for exchange of the actual key used to communicate during the current session. The following message is sent by the client that establishes one or two session keys with the server:

CLIENT-SESSION-KEY

The fourth phase is the *Server Verify* phase. This phase is used only when the RSA key exchange algorithm is used. It verifies the master key and the subsequent session keys obtained by the server. Upon receiving the master key and subsequent session keys from the client, the server decrypts the keys using its own private key. Next, the server sends a confirmation to the client by responding to the random challenge sent to it by the client in the CLIENT-HELLO message. The client decrypts the response to random challenge, and if everything matches, a trusted session is established between the client and the server. The following message is exchanged during this phase:

SERVER-VERIFY

The fifth phase is the *Client Authentication* phase. If client authentication is required, then the server asks the client for a certificate. The client responds with a *CLIENT-CERTIFICATE*. As of this writing, SSL supports only X.509 certificates (described in Chapter 5). The following messages are exchanged during this phase:

> REQUEST-CERTIFICATE
> CLIENT-CERTIFICATE

The sixth and final phase is the *finished* phase. In this phase, both the client and the server exchange their respective finished messages. The client indicates completion of authentication by sending the session ID as encrypted text. The server sends a *SERVER-FINISHED* message. This message includes the session ID encrypted with the master key. A trusted session is now established between the client and the server. The following messages are exchanged in this phase:

> CLIENT-FINISHED
> SERVER-FINISHED

SSL Record Protocol

The *SSL Record Protocol* specifies encapsulation of all transmitted and received data. The data portion of SSL record is composed of three components:

- MAC-DATA

- ACTUAL-DATA

- PADDING-DATA

The MAC-DATA is the *message authentication code*. For MD2 and MD5, this field is 128 bits long. The ACTUAL-DATA is the application data (payload) to be transmitted. The PADDING-DATA is the data required to pad the message when a block cipher is used. When the SSL record is sent as cleartext, the MAC_DATA and PADDING-DATA fields are not included. The MAC-DATA is computed by applying the hash function on:

MAC-DATA = HASH(SECRET, ACTUAL-DATA, PADDING-DATA, SEQUENCE-NUMBER).

The contents of the SECRET field depend on the party that is sending the message and the type of encryption. The SEQUENCE-NUMBER is a counter maintained by the client and the server. For each transmission direction, two counters are maintained; one counter is kept by the sender and the other by the receiver. The counter is incremented by 1 every time a sender transmits a message. Each sequence number is a 32-bit unsigned number.

Encryption Algorithms

As part of the negotiations between the client and the server, the sender can identify the encryption algorithm it supports. SSL Version 2 and Version 3 support:

- RC4 128-bits and MD5

- RC4 128-bits (export 40-bits) and MD5

- RC2 128-bits CBC (Cipher Block Chaining) and MD5

- RC2 128-bits (export 40-bits) and MD5

- IDEA 128-bits CBC (Cipher Block Chaining) and MD5

- DES 64-bits CBC and MD5

- DES 192-bits EDE3 CBC (Triple-DES using Encrypt-Decrypt-Encrypt with Cipher Block Chaining) and MD5

MD5 is used as the hash function for computing the MAC. See Chapter 2 for details of these algorithms.

There are constraints on the size of encryption key for exporting software products. The export regulations will permit a key size of up to 40 bits, although certain exceptions may be permitted (see Chapter 2). SSL recommends the use of at least 128 bits key length with RC2 and RC4 for domestic use in the United States. For export purposes, only 40 bits of the key are kept secret; the remaining 88 bits are sent in the clear.

Secure Hypertext Transfer Protocol (S-HTTP)

Secure HyperText Transfer Protocol (S-HTTP) was developed by Enterprise Integration Technologies (EIT). This description of S-HTTP is based on the Internet Draft (Rescorla 1995). S-HTTP provides flexible security services for HTTP transactions. S-HTTP–aware clients can communicate with S-HTTP–oblivious servers and vice versa, although such transactions obviously would not utilize the security features of S-HTTP.

Through a process of negotiations between the client and the server, a variety of security enhancements and the associated algorithms are provided. For example, the user can select whether the request and the reply be signed, encrypted, or both. Any message may be signed, authenticated, encrypted, or any combination of these, including no protection. Key management mechanisms include manually shared-secrets such as passwords, public key exchange, and Kerberos ticket distribution. If digital signature support is selected, then the appropriate certificate should be attached. S-HTTP supports X.509 certificates and certificate chains, such as the one used in PEM.

The negotiations between the client and the server are conducted by exchanging formatted data. This data includes various security options that the originator would accept. The lines in the data should conform to the following rules:

<Line> := <Field> ':' <Key-val>(';',<Key-val>)*
<Key-val> := <Key> '=' <Value>(',' <Value>)*
<Key> := <Mode>'-'<Action>
<Mode> := 'orig' | 'recv'
<Action> := 'optional' | 'required' | 'refused'

The *<Mode>* value indicates whether the action is for a message originated at this agent or for a message received by this agent. The *agent* is the source of this formatted data.

The *<Action>* parameter specifies the action to be performed. The *recv-optional:* value implies that the receiver will process the security feature if the other party also uses it, but also will process messages without this feature. The *recv-required:* value means that the receiver will not process messages without this feature. The *recv-refused:* specifies that the receiver will not process messages with this security feature. In addition, for information originating at this agent, corresponding action values are specified. For example, *orig-required:* indicates that the agent will always generate this security feature.

The negotiation headers include options to select a variety of algorithms for each header line. There is a header line for each of the following items.

S-HTTP-Privacy-Domains

This header specifies the class of encryption algorithms as well as the packaging of data. The two values defined for this header are PEM and PKCS-7.[*]

For example,

> S-HTTP-Privacy-Domains: orig-required=pem;
> recv-optional=pem, pkcs-7

This line implies that the agent always generates PEM-compliant messages, but can read PEM or PKCS-7 messages.

S-HTTP-Certificate-Types

This line specifies the acceptable certificate format. Currently, S-HTTP permits the value of *X.509* for X.509 certificates.

S-HTTP-Key-Exchange-Algorithms

This line indicates the algorithms to be used for key exchange. The permitted values are *RSA, Outband, Inband,* and *Krb.* RSA

---

[*] PKCS-7 is a cryptographic message encapsulation format similar to PEM. PKCS-7 is defined by RSA, and uses OSI's Abstract Syntax Notation (ASN.1).

is used if enveloping of data uses RSA. Outband is specified if there will be some external arrangement. Inband and Krb are used when keys are specified directly between the client and the server.

S-HTTP-Signature-Algorithms

This header identifies the algorithm for digital signature. The two supported algorithms are *RSA* and *NIST-DSS*.

S-HTTP-Message-Digest-Algorithms

This line identifies the algorithm for providing data integrity using the hash functions. The supported algorithms are *RSA-MD2, RSA-MD5,* and *NIST-SHS*.

S-HTTP-Symmetric-Content-Algorithms

This line specifies the symmetric-key block cipher algorithm used to encrypt the data. The symmetric encryption algorithms for S-HTTP are:

DES-CBC: DES in Cipher Block Chaining (CBC) Mode.
DES-EDE-CBC: Two-key Triple-DES using EDE in outer CBC mode.
DES-EDE3-CBC: Three-key Triple-DES using EDE in outer CBC mode.
DESX-CBC: RSA's DESX in CBC mode.
IDEA-CFB: IDEA in Cipher Feedback Mode.
RC2-CBC: RC2 in CBC mode.

RC4
CDMF: IBM's CDMF in CBC mode.

S-HTTP-Symmetric-Header-Algorithms

This line provides a list of the symmetric-key encryption used to encrypt the headers:

DES-ECB: DES in Electronic Codebook (ECB) Mode.
DES-EDE-ECB: Two-key Triple-DES using EDE in ECB mode.
DES-EDE3-ECB: Three-key Triple-DES using EDE in ECB mode.
DESX-ECB: DESX (RSA's) in ECB mode.
IDEA-ECB: IDEA in ECB mode.
RC2-ECB: RC2 in CBC mode.
CDMF-ECB: IBM's CDMF in ECB mode.

MD2, MD5, NIST's SHS (Secure Hash Standard), and the encryption algorithms are outlined in Chapter 2. For additional details, see Ahuja (1996) or Schneier (1994).

S-HTTP-Privacy-Enhancements

This header line specifies the security enhancements associated with the messages. The possible values are *sign, encrypt,* and *auth.* These values indicate whether the messages are signed, encrypted, or authenticated, respectively.

Other header lines pertain to the specification of various keys and their symbolic names. See Rescorla (1995) for additional details on S-HTTP.

S-HTTP and SSL

As shown in Figure 6.2, S-HTTP and SSL use different approaches to provide security services for Web users. SSL executes a negotiation protocol to establish a secure socket level connection. The SSL security services are transparent to the user and the application.

S-HTTP protocols are integrated with HTTP. Here, the security services are negotiated through the headers and the attributes attached to the page. S-HTTP services are available only to HTTP connections, and the application (HTTP) is well aware of S-HTTP services.

Given that S-HTTP is at the application layer and SSL is at the sockets layer, it is conceivable to devise a combined approach for S-HTTP and SSL.

Private Communication Technology

The Private Communication Technology (PCT) is defined as an Internet Draft by Benaloh (1995); as such, this information should be used as *work-in-progress*. According to this document, PCT is designed to provide privacy between a client and a server, and to authenticate the server, and optionally, the client. PCT also supports message integrity using a hash-function–based message authentication code.

PCT protocol is quite similar to SSL, and PCT record format is compatible with SSL. According to Benaloh (1995), PCT differs from SSL primarily in the design of the handshake phase, as follows.

- The number of messages and message structures are shorter and simpler than SSL. To reconnect a session without client authentication, it takes one message in each direction. For any other type of session reconnection, there are no more than two messages sent in each direction.

- The negotiation phase for the cryptographic session has been extended to cover more protocol characteristics.

- Message authentication has been modified so that it uses different keys than the encryption keys. As such, the keys for message authentication may be longer than the encryption keys.

It also claims to have addressed a security hole in SSL's client authentication. A detailed description of PCT can be found in Benaloh (1995).

GSSAPI for Web Security

The topic of GSSAPI for Web security has been addressed in an Internet Draft Rosenthal (1995). This document is an Internet Draft and as such, should be treated as *work-in-progress*.

GSSAPI can be used to provide mutual authentication and data encryption capabilities in Web browsers and servers. This support can be used for any security mechanisms, since GSSAPI is independent of the underlying security schemes. We described GSSAPI in Chapter 2. GSSAPI can also be used to secure other applications such as SSL and S-HTTP, as shown previously in Figure 3.1.

The initial HTTP connection is strongly authenticated and the entire transaction is protected using GSSAPI services. GSSAPI protects the various types of HTTP transactions such as document retrievals, form submissions, and CGI results. The GSSAPI integrates the application level protocols (such as HTTP) and the formats (such as HTML) in such a way that they are isolated from the operational characteristics of the underlying security scheme (such as the cryptographic key sizes). In this way, the Web transactions are secured without impacting or modifying the HTTP/HTML constructs.

To begin, a Web client and a server must acquire their respective credentials. Next, the Web client/server security context is established using the appropriate GSSAPI calls. Once the security context is established, the Web client and server can exchange information in a secure manner using data integrity (GSS-SIGN and GSS_VERIFY) or data integrity and encryption using GSS-SEAL and GSS-UNSEAL.

This approach is described in detail in Rosenthal (1995). Details on GSSAPI can be found in Chapter 2; for additional details refer to Linn (1993b), Wray (1993), and Ahuja (1996).

Security for Digital Economy

---

*"Ready or not, Companies are getting Web'd for Commerce.
But Glitches remain—namely, Payment, Security, and Integration."*

Mary Brandel. "Uncommon Commerce." *Electronic Commerce Journal*; supplement to *ComputerWorld*. April 29, 1996. page 19.

"Plan well, invest wisely, Prepare to wait for profits."

Scott Leibs. "Doing Business on the Net." *NetGuide*. June 1995. page 48.

The concept of *electronic commerce, e-commerce,* or *online commerce* relates to selling goods or services over the Internet. An integral part of e-commerce is to make electronic payments over the Internet. In this chapter, we review various approaches for making online payments to support electronic commerce.

According to International Data Corporation with Connect, Inc. and quoted in ComputerWorld Electronic Commerce Journal (April 29, 1996, page 5), companies are spending from $840,000 to $1.25 million to develop Internet-based interactive electronic commerce, four times more than expected. The development takes one year, which is twice as long as expected.

Prior to setting up a business on the Internet, it is prudent to study the concept of e-commerce and determine the best way your business can benefit from it. Some of the ways to provide unique capabilities are:

- Provide abundance of information online since there is no real-time interactive session with the seller.

- Be accessible to customers, such as through fax or telephone. It is possible that the consumer may want to ask questions or make payments through other means.

- Be prepared to change, seek feedback from customers, and be patient in expecting profits from online commerce.

From the consumer viewpoint, several areas are inhibiting the success of online commerce:

- It is not easy to find the shops on the Internet. For example, it may be faster and convenient to order pizza by the phone through an interactive conversation than to log on a web site and order pizza.

- It is hard to compare the prices and qualities of goods. It may be more convenient to visit three dress shops and select the desired clothing than to search and access three shops online, find the exact goods, and compare their qualities and prices.

- It is hard to find a large number of consumers willing to spend a significant amount of money shopping on the Internet. Even though the Internet user community is now 20 to 30 million, the real shoppers willing to spend money on the Internet are in short supply.

- It is not as much fun to shop on the Internet compared to browsing through the shopping malls with water fountains, ice cream and soda shops. Admittedly, shopping on the Internet can often save time and possibly money.

Banking Network in Online Commerce

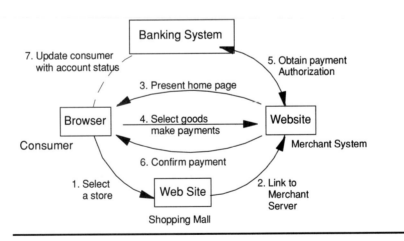

Figure 7.1: Banking System in Online Commerce

In Appendix C, we present details on online commerce. Figure 7.1 depicts an overview of the four elements of online commerce and their relationship to the banking network.

1. The consumer and the associated browser to interact with the consumer.

2. The merchant system residing on an online Web server with a connection to Web browsers over the Internet.

3. An online shopping mall that may help direct consumers to the merchant server.

4. The background banking network to support online payments from consumer to the merchant.

Consumer and the Browser

A consumer interacts with the online commerce system through a Web browser, described in Appendix B. Typically, the consumer first accesses a shopping mall and then uses the hyperlinks from the mall to access the merchant's home page.

The graphical display for the consumer should closely emulate the real shopping environment. So, it pays to present color graphics and 3D images. However, a typical home computer may have a 14.4 or 28.8 kilobits/s modem, and it may take a significantly long time to transfer color images to the home buyers.

Shopping Mall

A shopping mall is where most consumers first visit for a shopping spree. The connections between the shopping malls and a merchant's storefront are shown in Figure C.4 (see Appendix C). There will be several shopping malls, and it may pay to enlist with one or more well-known shopping malls. Typically, a merchant should be listed with several online shopping malls.

Merchant System

A merchant system consists of the home page and related software to manage the business. Details of a merchant system are depicted in Figure C.3 (see Appendix C).

Banking Network

The banking network consists of several components. First, there is a bank that processes the online financial transactions for the given merchant. This bank maintains the accounts for the merchant, authorizes and processes the payments. The merchant's bank also maintains a link with the consumer's bank for verifying the transactions. The link between the merchant and its bank is often real-time so as to allow online authorization of consumer payments. The consumer's bank typically has an offline link to the consumer, such as via postal mail or e-mail.

In short, the following steps are executed to complete a transaction, as shown in Figure 7.1.

1. The consumer accesses the shopping mall and selects a shop for purchasing certain items.

2. The shopping mall server accesses the merchant system for the selected shop.

3. The merchant system presents the store's home page to the consumer. It also includes information on the various goods available from this store.

4. The consumer selects the desired goods, interacts with the merchants system, and makes the payments. The topic of payment schemes is addressed later in this chapter and in Chapter 8.

5. The merchant system accesses its bank for authorization of the consumer payment. For this discussion, we will assume that the payment is authorized.

6. The merchant system informs the consumer that the payment is accepted and the transaction is completed. (At a later time, the merchant's bank obtains payment from the consumer's bank.)

7. The consumer's bank informs the consumer of the money transfer through mail such as a monthly report or online bank account.

The details on online commerce and the merchant system are presented in Appendix C.

Here, we address the topic of security for digital economy by reviewing various approaches for making payments to support online commerce.

Digital Economy

Basically, there are three primary ways in which consumers pay for their goods:

- Cash
- Checks
- Credit

However, there are other forms of payments that we are not addressing here, such as money orders, bank checks, debit cards, and traveler's checks. In addition, companies use lines of credit, purchase orders, and other methods to pay for goods.

In the following, we outline the concepts and basic approaches for deploying electronic cash, electronic checks, and electronic credit. We can design several variations and improvements to these schemes.

Note: There are certain banking and other regulations pertaining to handling electronic payments over the Internet. Such considerations are beyond the scope of this book and are not addressed here.

Electronic Cash

Electronic cash, e-cash, digital money, or *digital cash* provides the means to transfer money between parties over a network such as the Internet. Electronic cash must satisfy some general properties of digital money.

1. **Independence**: Electronic cash must not depend on its existence in any given computer system or location.

2. **Nonreusability**: Electronic cash should not be reusable after its first use. For example, if I get electronic cash for $50 and spend it to buy a shirt, then I cannot spend this money again.

3. **Anonymity**: Electronic cash cannot provide information that can be used to trace the previous owner of the cash. If I buy a shirt, there should be nothing associated with the electronic cash that traces it to me.

4. **Transferability**: Electronic cash should be easily transferable from one person or party to another. This should occur without leaving any trace of who has been in possession of this money.

5. **Divisibility**: Electronic cash must be available in several denominations. It should also be divisible in a way similar to real cash. For example, 25 digital pennies should yield a digital quarter and four digital quarters should equal a dollar.

6. **Secure Storage**: Electronic cash should be available in such a way so it can be securely stored at the consumer's hard drive, or on a smart card (such as a PCMCIA card). Furthermore, it should be possible to transfer this electronic cash between various types of parties on the Internet.

To begin, assume that there is an electronic cash-issuing bank that generates electronic cash. We will call such a bank or institution an *e-mint*. The e-mint signs the electronic cash as the issuer. It may use a digital signature algorithm such as those described in Chapter 2. The e-mint issues the electronic cash based on the funds provided to it by the customer. The payer (customer) can use this electronic cash to purchase items over the Internet. The e-mint may typically issue electronic money in denominations of one cent to $100, although other denominations are possible. It is also possible to generate electronic cash in other currencies.

Electronic Cash System

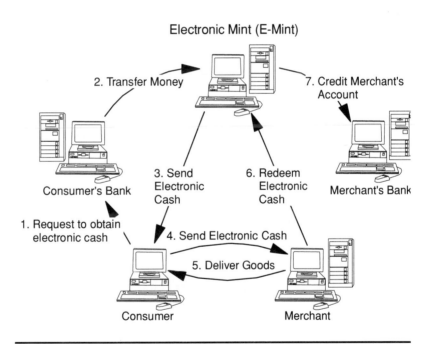

Figure 7.2: Electronic Cash System

Figure 7.2 depicts the elements for an electronic cash system. For simplicity, we are not including the online shopping malls. The electronic cash transactions take place in three distinct and independent phases.

Phase I: Obtaining Electronic Cash

This phase is depicted in steps 1 through 3 of Figure 7.2.

1. The consumer requests his or her bank to transfer money to the e-mint to obtain electronic cash.

2. The consumer's bank transfers money from the consumer's account to the e-mint.

3. The e-mint sends electronic cash to the consumer. The consumer saves the electronic cash on a hard drive or a smart card.

Phase II: Purchasing with Electronic Cash

This phase is executed whenever the consumer desires to make a purchase with electronic cash. It can take place at any time after the consumer has obtained electronic cash from the e-mint. A consumer can make purchases more than once as long as he or she does not run out of electronic cash.

4. The consumer selects the goods and transfers the electronic cash to the merchant.

5. The merchant provides the goods to the consumer.

Details on the interactions with the merchant were depicted and addressed earlier in Figure 7.1.

Phase III: Redeeming Cash by the Merchant

This phase occurs whenever the merchant is ready to redeem the electronic cash. The merchant should be capable of converting this electronic cash to money for the merchant's bank account.

6. The merchant transfers the electronic cash to the e-mint. Alternatively, the merchant may send the electronic cash to its bank, and the bank in turn redeems the money from the e-mint.

7. The e-mint transfers money to the merchant's bank for crediting the merchant's account.

Finally, note that this example shows the exchange of electronic cash between a customer and a merchant. However, a similar scheme can be devised to transfer money between two individuals or institutions such as banks, universities, or other businesses.

Security Schemes for Electronic Cash

There are four aspects to security for electronic cash relating to its generation, authenticity, distribution, and storage.

Generation of Electronic Cash

The electronic cash system must be capable of generating electronic cash including unique identifiers such as the serial numbers on dollar bills. According to MarkTwain (1995), for Mark

Twain's bank, a customer buys the electronic cash from a bank by drawing money from his or her checking account. The customer's computer also generates and sends random binary number(s) of 64-bits or higher. The bank removes the encryption envelope from the customer, checks and records the number(s), and digitally signs and sends it to the customer. The message includes the customer's binary numbers, and each number represents a certain amount of cash. The customer can send this electronic cash to any vendor in order to purchase goods. The vendor can then go to the bank, where the serial number of the customer's electronic cash is checked. If the serial numbers are verified, the vendor receives the money.

Authenticity

The electronic cash is digitally signed by the private key of the e-mint. The receiver uses the e-mint's public key to decrypt the electronic cash. In this way, the receiver is assured that the electronic cash was signed by the owner of the private key, which should be an authorized e-mint. For a receiver to obtain the public key of the e-mint, the X.509 certificate of the e-mint may be attached with the electronic cash. Alternatively, the public keys of e-mints may be well publicized to prevent any fraud.

Transporting Electronic Cash

For transportation, electronic cash must be secured and reliably transported. The electronic cash can be secured by encrypting it. The integrity of the electronic cash can be preserved by computing and attaching an encrypted message digest. In this way, it can be ensured that the electronic cash was not tampered with during transmission.

To reliably transport the data, the end-to-end protocols need to allow for recovery from loss of packets; for example, electronic cash that has been lost due to failure of a node in the Internet. Then the end nodes should be capable of retransmitting the packet, and should avoid duplicate receipts of the packet and dual existence of electronic cash on the Internet. TCP/IP protocols address some of the reliability issues, as described in Appendix A.

Storage of Electronic Cash

Finally, another security concern with electronic cash relates to securing the electronic cash file. If an electronic check (described later) is stolen or lost, then you can request to stop the payment. When an electronic cash file is lost, you potentially may lose the money. The users and the banks must have a secure way of storing the electronic cash so that it cannot be stolen. Given that all the transactions are conducted online, it is conceivable to track and decline payments when stolen cash is being used. Another approach to address this concern is for users to carry smart cards that carry electronic cash. Smart cards are described later in this chapter.

Benefits and Concerns

There are certain benefits and risks to electronic cash.

1. The potential for fraud is reduced. When the bank receives the electronic cash and verifies the serial number, it deletes the number and takes it out of cir-

culation forever. As such, you cannot copy the number and use it again.

2. Merchants would prefer an electronic cash scheme, since it prevents denial by the customer or lack of funds in a customer's account. In the case of a credit card or check payment, the customer can refuse or stop payment.

3. It can protect the customer's anonymity so that although the merchant is assured of the payment, the merchant does not need to know the details of the customer. However, on the Internet, the merchant may require the customer's name and address to deliver the goods.

There are certain concerns to be addressed for an electronic cash system. For example, who has the right to issue electronic cash? Can every bank issue its own money? If so, how do you prevent fraud? How will things such as coupons be handled? Who will monitor the banking operations to protect the consumers? Many of these concerns relate to the legal and banking regulatory aspects that are not addressed here. Those aspects are beyond the scope of this book but must be addressed before establishing a complete digital payment system.

Electronic Checks and Funds Transfer

Electronic funds transfer has been in existence for several years. It has consisted of three forms of transactions:

- Paying fees through the ATM (automatic teller machine) network

- Paying bills through monthly bank account deductions

- Transfer of large sums of money among banks across the world

Electronic checking pertains to the use of networking services to issue and process payments that emulate real-world checking. The payer issues a digital check to the payee, and the payee deposits it in the bank to redeem the money. Each transaction is carried over the Internet.

Electronic checking differs from electronic funds transfer in several ways. For electronic checking, electronic versions of checks are issued, received, and processed. So, the payee issues an electronic check for each payment. For electronic funds transfer, automatic withdrawals are made for monthly bills or other fixed payments; no checks are issued.

Electronic Check System

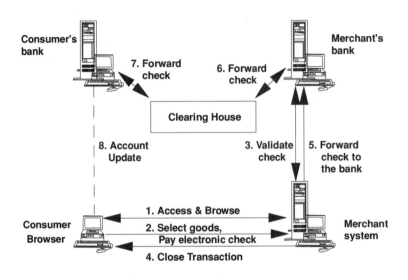

Figure 7.3: An Electronic Check system

The concept of *electronic checking* or *e-checks* can be described using Figure 7.3. In case of electronic cash, we outlined five primary parties: the consumer, the merchant, the consumer's bank, the merchant's bank, and the e-mint. For e-checks, we have added the *clearing house* to process checks among different banks. The functions described for a clearing house may be handled by a separate entity or by an existing banking system. For simplicity, we have not included the online malls.

The consumer uses a Web browser that has access to various Web servers over the Internet. The consumer views various shopping malls and storefronts at the browser. The browser has provisions for displaying the electronic check formats. The banks process electronic checks that are similar to paper checks.

A complete electronic check transaction may consist of several basic steps outlined next. These steps are executed in three distinct and optionally separate phases. In the first phase, the consumer makes a purchase. In the second phase, the merchant sends the electronic checks to its bank for redemption. In the third phase, the merchant's bank approaches the clearing house or the consumer's bank to cash the electronic checks.

Phase I: Purchasing Goods

1. The consumer accesses the merchant server, and the merchant server presents its goods to the consumer.

2. The consumer selects the goods and purchases them by sending an electronic check to the merchant.

3. The merchant may validate the electronic check with its bank for payment authorization.

4. Assuming the check is validated, the merchant closes the transaction with the consumer.

Phase II: Depositing Checks at the Merchant's Bank

5. The merchant electronically forwards the checks to its bank. This action takes place at the discretion of the merchant.

Phase III: Clearing the Checks Among the Banks

6. The merchant's bank forwards the electronic checks to the clearing house for cashing.

7. The clearing house works with the consumer's bank, clears the check, and transfers money to the merchant's bank, which updates the merchant's account.

8. At a later time, the consumer's bank updates the consumer with the withdrawal information.

Security Schemes for Electronic Checks

The security requirements for electronic checks consist of authenticating the electronic check, supplying the originator's public key to the receiver, and securely storing the originator's private key.

Authenticity of Electronic Checks

The electronic check may consist of a document that is signed by the consumer's private key. The receiver (the merchant or the merchant's bank) uses the payer's public key to decrypt the digital signature. This assures the receiver that the sender indeed signed the check. It also provides for nonrepudiation, such that the payer cannot deny issuing the check since it is signed by the payer's private key (that only the payer is expected to possess).

Additionally, the electronic check also may require the digital signatures of the originator's bank. This step will assure the receiver that the check is written on a valid bank account. The receiver (or receiver's bank) can validate the authenticity of the originator's bank by using the public key of the originator's bank.

For large sums of money, additional security requirements may be levied.

Delivering Public Keys

The originator as well as the originator's bank must provide their public keys to the receiver. The public keys can be provided by attaching their X.509 certificates (see Chapter 5) to the electronic checks. These certificates may use certificate chains including the signatures of the root CA. The public key of the root CA should be well publicized to avoid fraud.

Storage of Private Keys

To avoid fraud, the consumer's private key needs to be securely stored and made available to the consumer. This can be achieved by providing a smart card that the consumer can carry. The topic of smart cards is presented later in this chapter.

Cashier's Checks

Finally, a cashier's check may be issued by a bank as follows. The check is created by a bank and is signed using the bank's private key. The originating bank includes its certificate with the electronic check. The receiving bank uses the originating bank's public key to decrypt the digital signature. In this way, the receiving bank is assured that the cashier check indeed was originated by the name of the bank indicated on the check. It also provides the receiving bank with nonrepudiation such that the originating bank cannot deny issuing this check since it is signed by the originating bank's private key (that only the orig-inating bank is expected to possess).

This electronic checking approach is simply an outline of some of the basic steps and the potential use of public key cryptosys-tem for data origin authentication and digital signature. A comprehensive electronic checking system over the Internet will require a detailed system design along with associated security issues that are not covered here.

Benefits and Concerns

Compared to paper checks and other forms of payments, elec-tronic checking provides the following advantages:

Time Saved: Electronic checks can be issued without needing to fill out, mail, or deliver checks. It also saves time in process-ing the checks. With paper checks, the merchant collects all the checks and deposits them at the merchant's bank. With elec-tronic checks, the merchant instantly can forward checks to the bank and get them credited to their account. As such, e-checks can greatly reduce the time from the moment a consumer writes a check to the time when the merchant receives the deposit.

Reduced Paper Handling Cost: There is no need for long lines at the banks on the first day of the month, or for long lines of students paying their tuition at the university. Correspondingly, it reduces the bank employees' effort to receive the checks, pro-cess them, and mail the cancelled checks to the consumers.

Reduction in Bounced Checks: Electronic checking can be designed in such a way that the merchant can get authorization from the customer's bank before accepting the electronic check.

This approach could be similar to the cashier's check approach described earlier.

Electronic checks can be used to give gifts or make payments without the fear of being lost or stolen. If a check is stolen, the receiver can request the payer to stop the payment. On the other hand, electronic cash is exposed to theft and other risks.

Electronic checks do not require secure storage such as that required for electronic cash. However, it still requires secure storage of the consumer's private key.

There are some privacy issues to be addressed for e-checks, as discussed in Panurach (1996). The check must pass through the banking system. However, the banking system is obligated to document the details of every transaction passing through the system. While maintaining such records, the banks need to protect the payee's privacy and not divulge the details of banking transactions.

Electronic Credit

The third and final digital economy scheme is using credit cards for electronic commerce. In electronic credit, conventional credit cards may be used along with a PIN. The PIN is a secret code that the consumer must enter while using the credit card online. As such, it prevents misuse of the credit card in case it is stolen.

Electronic Credit System

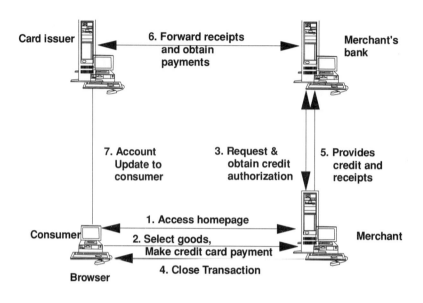

Figure 7.4: An Electronic Credit system

Figure 7.4 depicts a conceptual approach for using credit cards to purchase goods and services on the Internet. Similar to the previous approaches, electronic credit uses four essential components. For simplicity, we have not included the online shopping mall in this discussion.

1. A consumer along with a Web browser, as described earlier for other digital economy schemes.

2. A merchant server that provides the home page. Specifically, the merchant server handles the credit card transactions.

3. A merchant's bank that handles the credit card transactions for the merchant.

4. A card-issuing institution that has issued a credit
card to the consumer.

An electronic credit card transaction processes the following
steps, which can be divided into three phases. The first phase
completes the purchase of goods by the consumer. The second
phase completes the transfer of money from the consumer
account to the merchant. The third phase informs the consumer
about the charges and deductions to his or her account.

Phase I: Purchase of Goods

1. The consumer accesses a merchant's home page and
receives a display of the merchant's goods.

2. The consumer selects the desired goods and offers a
credit card payment to the merchant.

3. The merchant server accesses its bank for credit
authorization of the consumer's credit card number
and the amount of purchase. The merchant's bank
completes the authorization and informs the merchant whether to proceed with the purchase.

4. The merchant informs the consumer whether the
transaction has been completed.

Phase II: Settlement

This phase is executed separately by the merchant server to col-
lect the payments on various credit card purchases.

5. The merchant server accesses the merchant's bank and provides a collection of receipts of various electronic credit purchases.

6. The merchant's bank accesses the card issuer and obtains the money for the purchases.

Phase III: Consumer Update of Credit Card Bill

7. In this phase, the card issuer updates the card holder (consumer) about the amount of credit transferred to other parties as a result of the purchases. The consumer may receive the account updates once a month through postal mail.

Security Schemes for Electronic Credit

There are the following security requirements for electronic credit card transactions.

1. It must provide a mechanism to validate the identity of the merchant's bank, the merchant, and the consumer. A fraud can potentially result from whichever party is not sufficiently authenticated. X.509 certificates may be sent with each message to authenticate the sender and to provide the sender's public key.

2. It must protect the private key of the certificate authority (see Chapter 5). Theft or loss of the CA's private key can cause significant damage.

3. It must protect the credit card number, the expiration date, PIN, the amount of purchase, and other sensitive information during transmission over the Internet.

4. It must institute a process to resolve credit card payment disputes between the consumer, the merchant, and the bank.

A comprehensive scheme to provide electronic credit has been designed and published for public comments. Secure Electronic Transaction (SET) is described in the next chapter.

Benefits and Concerns

Electronic credit approach has the following benefits.

1. The credit card number and expiration date can be prevented from disclosure to the merchant. This characteristic does not exist in the traditional credit card systems. In this context, the electronic credit can provide a higher level of security than traditional credit card systems.

2. The electronic credit system can be designed to obtain almost instant payments to the merchants from credit card sales. For traditional credit card systems, it takes significant time for the merchant to deliver the credit card receipts to the bank, and for the bank to settle the payments.

Some of the concerns to be addressed for electronic credit transactions are:

1. A procedure will be required to handle any loss of credit card information over the Internet.

2. The electronic card system must provide nonrepudiation and related documentation to address any disputes. The credit card receipts are generated electronically. As such, any disputes should be resolvable based on available online documentation.

Smart Cards

Smart cards are credit-card size cards that can be carried in a wallet. These cards have a processor and memory on the card. In this way, digital cash or private keys can be stored on the cards and can be carried around by the consumer. Sometimes, these cards are referred to as PCMCIA cards, since the card may be designed to fit in the PCMCIA slots of a computer.

There are four types of microcircuit cards that can be used as smart cards, according to Lynch (1996).

Memory Cards

Memory cards contain space for data storage. These cards can be used to store passwords or PIN. Many telephone cards use these memory cards.

Shared-Key Cards

Shared-key cards can store a private key such as those used in public key cryptosystems. In this way, the user can plug in the card to a workstation, and the workstation can read the private key for encryption or decryption. Some cards may also process encryption algorithms such as DES.

Signature-Carrying Cards

Signature-carrying cards contain a set of pregenerated random numbers. These numbers can be used to generate electronic cash.

Signature-Creating Cards

Signature-creating cards carry a coprocessor that can be used to generated large random numbers. These random numbers then can be used for assignment as serial numbers for electronic cash.

The signature-carrying cards and the signature-creating cards can be used to generate electronic cash by a user. The user then sends this cash securely to a bank, the bank draws money from the user's account and then issues the cash under its name by adding the bank's signatures.

Details on smart cards can be found in Lynch (1996). The topic of digital economy for electronic commerce is relatively new. Some of the related references include Panurach (1996), Bakel (1996), Lynch (1996), Wayner (1996), and Loshin (1995).

Secure Payment Protocols and Systems

"Transforming money from bills in your wallet into charged electrons on your hard disk is probably a greater abstract leap than the transformation of gold coins to flat currency."

Patiwat Panurach, "Money in Electronic Commerce: Digital Cash, Electronic Fund Transfer, and Ecash," *Communications of the ACM*. June 1996, V39. no.6. p. 50.

Internet commerce relies on an underlying secure payment scheme. The payment scheme may involve a variety of participating parties and payment methods. In Chapter 7, we discussed some of the payment schemes and the related security issues. In this chapter, we discuss the protocols and systems that support secure payment schemes for electronic commerce. Before proceeding to describe some of the common secure payment protocols, we must first review the elements and the architecture for secure payments.

Secure Payment Architecture

A secure payment scheme for electronic commerce must support the following features.

1. Strong authentication of each party using X.509 certificate and digital signature.

2. Privacy of transactions using encryption.

3. Transaction integrity using message digest algorithms.

4. Nonrepudiation to handle disputes about the transaction.

5. Multiparty payment protocol among the various parties transacting electronic commerce.

Authentication

To achieve a secure protocol, an important requirement is to validate the identity of each party transacting electronic commerce. For example, the consumer must authenticate itself to the merchant and the bank, the merchant must authenticate itself to the consumer and the bank, and so on. To offer such authentication, we will use the concepts and approaches for X.509 certificates presented in Chapter 5.

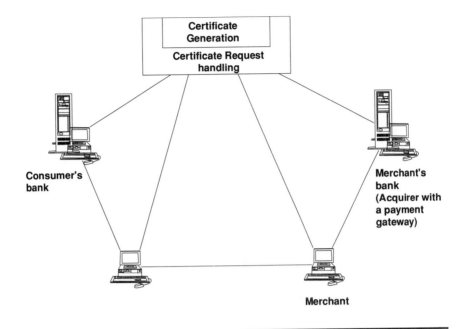

Figure 8.1: Certification for secure payments

Figure 8.1 depicts the basic components for transacting payments on the Internet. The merchant's bank is also called an *acquirer,* and represents a financial institution that has an account with a merchant and processes bank-card authorizations and payment. A *payment gateway* is a device operated by an acquirer to handle merchant payment messages. An important component for secure payments is the certificate authority. The certificate authority issues X.509 certificates to various parties. There may also be a registration authority residing with some of the merchant's banks. The registration authority provides the certificates for the merchants that they can use to demonstrate to the consumer that it is a legitimate merchant. Clearly, the registration authority needs to work in concert with the certificate authority. This concept is similar to the certificate chains described in Chapter 5.

Privacy and Data Integrity

To support transaction privacy, the protocol must support some of the encryption schemes. While using the Web browsers and servers, the protocol can utilize the Secure Sockets Layer (SSL) or Secure HypterText Transfer Protocol (S-HTTP). Depending on the requirements, symmetric key encryption or asymmetric key encryption can be used. Data encryption and data integrity can be provided by deploying the encryption and message digest algorithms described in Chapter 2.

Nonrepudiation

Nonrepudiation can be established through the use of public-key schemes and the X.509 certificates. To initiate a transaction, a given party sends its X.509 certificate to the other party. The recipient determines the public key of the sender from the certificate. In addition, each message can be protected by applying the MD5 one-way hash algorithm. The message digest can be encrypted using the sender's private key. Next, the sender can compute a new symmetric encryption key every time a new message is to be sent. The message can be encrypted using this new symmetric encryption key. The symmetric encryption key can be sent to the recipient by encrypting it with sender's private key. In this way, the receiver can establish that the sender indeed sent a given message. It also provides additional security through the use of symmetric key encryption.

Multiparty Protocol

A multiparty secure payment scheme should address the following additional issues:

- The merchant should have access to only the order information, such as the types of goods and the sale prices. The merchant should not require access to the consumer's credit card information as long as the acquirer (merchant's bank) authorizes the payment.

- The merchant's bank is exposed to only the payment information. In general, there is no need for the bank to know the details of the goods purchased. There may be exceptions when someone buys an expensive item such as a car or a house.

These requirements offer security enhancements to the traditional payment schemes, such as the credit card schemes. There also may be some banking regulations and legal requirements that are beyond the scope of the book and are not addressed here.

Secure Payment Protocols

In the last few years, some payment schemes have emerged. These schemes use a variety of payment protocols and implementations. In the following, we review some of the common (secure) payment protocols and systems for electronic commerce:

- iKP protocols

- Secure Electronic Transactions (SET) protocols

- First Virtual

- CyberCash

- Mark Twain Bank

iKP Protocols

IBM Research Division has designed a family of protocols to securely transfer payments over the Internet. This work was presented at the USENIX Workshop on Electronic Commerce in July 1995 (Bellare 1995). The iKP scheme is also described in Wayner (1996). The most significant feature of this scheme is that it provides complete cryptographic protection of data including an audit trail to resolve disputes. The iKP scheme arbitrates payment information among three parties, compared to the two-party SSL and S-HTTP protocols. It is based on RSA public-key scheme and can be extended for debit card or electronic check models of payment.

Three parties are involved directly in a payment transaction: the customer, the merchant, and the *acquirer gateway* (or *gateway*). The gateway is the front-end code that interfaces for the merchant's bank. The customer makes the payment and the merchant receives the payment. The acquirer gateway interfaces with the existing payment infrastructure and authorizes the transaction by using the existing infrastructure.

The iKP stands for i-Key-Protocol, i = 1, 2, or 3. The value of i determines the number of parties that hold their public/private key pairs. So, *1KP* is the simplest protocol where only the acquirer gateway possesses the public/private key pair. For *2KP*, the acquirer gateway as well as the merchant server possess the public/private key pair. Finally, the *3KP* protocols require each of the three parties to possess the public/private key pairs. Clearly, 3KP protocol offers the highest level of security, and 1KP protocol offers the lowest level of security in this scheme.

In the case of 1KP, the customer and the merchant are not required to possess the public/private key pair. However, the customer as well as the merchant must be capable of ensuring the authenticity of the gateway. To do that, the customer and the merchant are provided with the public key of the certification authority (CA) that issues a certificate to the acquirer gateway. So when customers or merchants receive an X.509 certificate from the acquirer gateway, they can use the CA's public key to decrypt the certificate. A successful decryption of the certificate also implies that the certificate was indeed issued by the appropriate CA. Since there would not be too many gateways, the credit card company may issue these certificates. In this 1KP scheme, the customers are authenticated by their credit card number and possibly the PIN (Personal Identification Number). Although this scheme is simple, it does not offer nonrepudiation of messages sent by the customer or the merchant. As such, this scheme does not provide some of the means to resolve disputes relating to the authenticity of the payment.

For the 2KP protocol, the merchant as well as the gateway possess the public/private key pairs. So this protocol provides nonrepudiation of messages originated by the merchant and the gateway. It also enables the customer and the gateway to ensure that they are dealing with a legitimate merchant.

The 3KP protocol provides nonrepudiation of messages from all three parties. Payment orders are authenticated by the digital signature, the credit card number, and (optionally) the PIN number. According to Bellare (1995), this makes the forging of payment orders computationally infeasible. Finally, note that each customer, merchant, and the gateway require a public/ private key pair. So for this scheme, an infrastructure will be required to issue X.509 certificates to all the parties, such as the one shown in Figure 8.1.

Secure Electronic Transactions (SET)

"The Stage is 'SET'—The SET agreement between MasterCard and Visa could pave the way for wide-spread e-commerce."

Larry Loeb. *Internet World.* August 1996. page 55.

In February 1996, it was reported that MasterCard and Visa had agreed to jointly develop a technical standard for secure payments over the Internet. Before this agreement, MasterCard and Visa each were developing separate protocols for transacting secure credit card business over the Internet. MasterCard was working with Netscape and IBM to design SEPP (Secure Electronic Payment Protocol) and Visa was working with Microsoft to design STT (Secure Transaction Technology), according to Loeb (1996).

A Secure Electronic Transaction (SET) specification was published on February 23, 1996. Although revisions are underway, this is one of the most comprehensive documents that describes the various aspects of credit card payments over the

Internet. According to the document, the specification was jointly developed by MasterCard and Visa; advice and assistance was provided by GTE, IBM, Microsoft, Netscape, SAIC, Terisa, and Verisign. The following description is based primarily on MCVISA (1996). This description is necessarily brief and does not cover all the details. For additional details, refer to MCVISA (1996).

Business Requirements

SET addresses the following business requirements, according to MCVISA (1996):

1. Provide confidentiality of payment information and facilitate confidentiality of the order information accompanying the payment information.

2. Ensure data integrity for all transmitted information.

3. Provide authentication of a cardholder (consumer) as a legitimate user of a branded bank-card account.

4. Provide authentication so that a merchant can accept payments from a branded bank-card account through the merchant's relationship with an acquiring financial institution.

5. Ensure the best system design and security practices to protect all legitimate parties of an electronic commerce transaction.

6. Ensure the development of a protocol that is neither dependent on nor prevents the use of an underlying transport security mechanism.

7. Facilitate and encourage interoperability among providers of software and networks.

Features

We describe the SET features in the context of these requirements.

Confidentiality of Information

It is important that the cardholder account and payment information is transmitted securely without being accessible to
unauthorized parties. A potential fraud can occur by an
intruder intercepting all traffic and filtering the account information, such as the credit card number, expiration data, and
the cardholder name.

Data confidentiality is ensured through the use of message
encryption.

Data Integrity

The payment protocol must ensure that the message content is
not modified during transmission between the sender and the
receiver. The payment information from the sender (cardholder) includes personal data, order information, and instructions for the payment. SET must provide the means to ensure
that the message content is protected from any modifications.

Data integrity is provided through the use of digital signatures.

Authentication of Cardholder Account

The payment protocol should furnish the means for a merchant to ensure that a given customer is a legitimate user. Specifically, the cardholder must be authenticated to be a legitimate user of a valid branded bank-card account number.

The cardholder authentication is achieved through the use of the cardholder certificate and the digital signatures.

Merchant Authentication

The payment protocol must also specify the means for a given merchant to be authenticated to a cardholder. In particular, the cardholder must have a mechanism to confirm that the merchant has a relationship with some banking institution that permits the merchant to accept bank-card payments.

Merchant authentication is provided through the use of digital signatures and merchant certificates.

Interoperability

The payment protocols must provide the capability that it can operate on a variety of hardware and software platforms without providing preference to one over another.

Interoperability is provided by the use of specific protocols and message formats.

Steps for Electronic Shopping

SET describes the following steps for an electronic shopping experience.

1. The cardholder accesses the merchant information and browses for items. The cardholder may browse a paper catalog, a catalog supplied on a CD-ROM, or a catalog on the merchant's Web page.

2. The cardholder chooses items for purchase.

3. The cardholder is presented an order form. This form includes the list of items selected by the cardholder for purchase. The form also includes the prices of the selected items and the total price. The form can either be provided by the merchant server or created by the shopping software at the browser.

4. The cardholder selects the form of payment. The cardholder may choose to make the payment through electronic cash, electronic check, or electronic credit. The SET specifications focus on the use of credit card payments.

5. The cardholder verifies the list of items and identifies the form of payment. SET specifies that the cardholder software digitally sign the order and payment instructions.

6. The merchant requests and obtains payment authorization from the cardholder's financial institution that issued the card.

7. The merchant confirms the order to the cardholder.

8. The merchant ships the items or performs services purchased by the cardholder.

9. The merchant requests for payment from the card-holder's financial institution.

According to MCVISA (1996), the SET specifications focus on steps 5, 6, 7, and 9 under the option to use the bank-card payment.

Payment Processing

The SET specifications provide details on processing of various payment transactions. The primary payment transactions consist of the following:

- Cardholder registration
- Merchant registration
- Purchase request
- Payment authorization
- Payment capture

The cardholder and the merchant obtain their certificates prior to transacting business. The purchase request, payment authorization, and payment capture correspond to steps 5, 6, 7, and 9.

These transactions use the public/private key pairs as well as symmetric key encryption. Messages are often encrypted using a newly generated random symmetric encryption key. This key is transmitted to the receiver after encrypting it using the receiver's public key.

We will review parts of the first three transactions next. There are other transactions not included in our description such as certificate query, sale transaction, and authorization reversal. Complete details on all these transactions can be found in MCVISA (1996).

Cardholder Registration

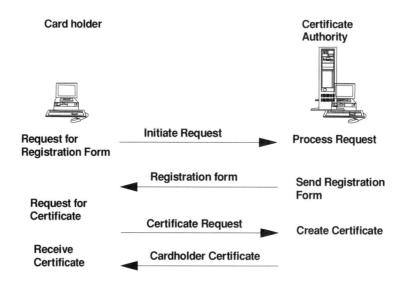

Figure 8.2: Cardholder Registration

To begin, the cardholder must possess the public key of the certificate authority (CA). The CA has two public/private key pairs. One key pair is used for key exchange, and the other key pair is used for digital signatures.

The cardholder needs a copy of the registration form from the card-issuing financial institution. The registration process, shown in Figure 8.2, begins by the cardholder requesting the CA's key-exchange certificate and the registration form. The cardholder also identifies the card-issuing financial institution to the CA.

The CA receives the request from the cardholder. It identifies the financial institution from the request and selects the appropriate form to be sent to the cardholder. CA sends the registration form along with the CA's own key-exchange certificate to the cardholder.

The cardholder verifies the CA certificate. It traverses the trust chain to verify the CA's authenticity. The trust chain comes from a trust tree with a "root certificate authority" and other CAs. Each CA in the trust tree has been designated by the root CA, directly or through other authorities, to issue certificates (see Figure 5.5).

The cardholder uses two sets of public/private key pairs. One key pair is used for key exchange and the other for digital signatures. The key exchange is used only during the certificate processing.

The cardholder fills out the registration form. The form includes details such as the name, address, and expiration date. Next, the software at the cardholder performs the following functions:

- It digitally signs the registration message.
- It generates a random symmetric encryption key.
- It uses this random key to encrypt the registration message.
- It encrypts the random key and the account number into a digital envelope using the CA public key-

exchange key. As such, only the appropriate CA can decrypt this information.

- It transmits these components to the CA.

Upon receiving this information, the CA performs the following actions:

- It decrypts the digital envelope using the CA's private key.

- It obtains the symmetric encryption key from the decrypted message.

- It uses the symmetric encryption key to decrypt the registration request.

- It uses the signature key in the message to verify if the corresponding private key was used to sign the message. If the message is verified and the CA accepts the information in the registration request, then the processing continues. Otherwise, the user request is rejected.

- It creates and signs a digital certificate for the cardholder.

- It creates a new random encryption key.

- It encrypts the certificate using this new random encryption key.

- It encrypts the random encryption key using the cardholder's public key-exchange key. As such, only the cardholder can decrypt the random encryption key.

When the cardholder software receives this response from the CA, it performs the following actions:

- It decrypts the random encryption key using cardholder's private key.
- It decrypts the registration response using the random encryption key and extracts the certificate.
- It verifies the certificate and stores it for future use.

Merchant Registration

The merchant registration essentially follows the same steps as the cardholder registration. The merchant software performs actions similar to those performed by the cardholder software. For the sake of simplicity, we skip the details.

Purchase Request

Figure 8.3 depicts the basic flows for a purchase request.

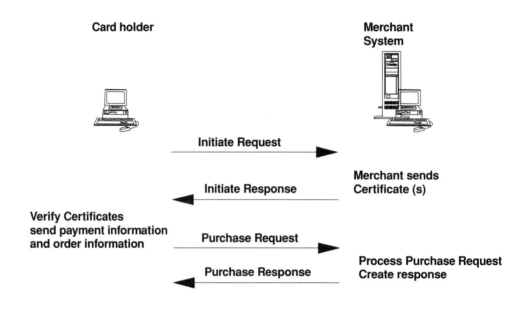

Card holder

Merchant System

Initiate Request →

Initiate Response ←   **Merchant sends Certificate (s)**

Verify Certificates send payment information and order information

Purchase Request →

Purchase Response ←   **Process Purchase Request Create response**

Figure 8.3: Purchase Request

The cardholder has browsed and selected the items. The cardholder must have already obtained the merchant's public key-exchange key and the payment gateway's key-exchange key. This transaction starts by the cardholder requesting a copy of the merchant's certificate and the payment gateway's certificate. The cardholder includes information about the bank-card brand that will be used for this transaction.

When the merchant software receives this request, it performs the following actions:

- It assigns a unique transaction identifier to the message.

- It transmits the merchant's certificate and the payment gateway's certificate that correspond to the bank-card brand. It also includes the transaction identifier.

Upon receiving this response, the cardholder software performs following actions:

- It verifies the merchant certificate and the gateway certificates by traversing the trust chain.
- It verifies the merchant signature by decrypting it with the merchant's public signature key. It computes a new hash of the response and compares it with the decrypted hash in the response.
- It creates the Order Information (OI) and the Payment Instructions (PI).
- It includes the cardholder signature certificate with the OI.
- It computes a dual message digest as follows. It computes a message digest each for the PI and the OI. These message digests are concatenated and a new message digest is computed from the result. The resulting dual hash is encrypted using the cardholder private signature key.
- It generates a random symmetric encryption key.
- It encrypts the dual-signed PI with the random symmetric encryption key.
- It encrypts the random symmetric encryption key and the cardholder account number into a digital envelope using the Payment Gateway's key-exchange key. As such, only the payment gateway can decrypt the payment information.
- It transmits a message consisting of the PI and OI to the merchant.

The merchant server software performs the following actions after receiving this message:

- It verifies the cardholder certificate by traversing the trust chain to the root key.

- It verifies the message digest as follows. It decrypts the dual signature by using the cardholder public signature key. It generates a new hash of the concatenation of the two message digests and compares the result with the decrypted dual digest. If the results match, then the message integrity is verified.

- It processes the request and forwards the PI to the payment gateway for authorization.

- It creates a purchase response and includes the merchant certificate.

- It generates a message digest and digitally signs it using the merchant's private signature key.

- It transmits the response to the cardholder.

The SET specifications are undergoing revisions and therefore subject to change. We briefly have reviewed some of the security aspects; complete details can be found in MCVISA (1996) or its later revisions. Several vendors have stated their intentions to implement SET and some prototypes have been demonstrated at Internet conferences.

First Virtual

The First Virtual Holdings, Inc. is designed to provide complete commercial transactions on the Internet. It uses e-mail to transfer information among various parties with a clearinghouse. The clearinghouse interprets correctly formatted e-mail messages and transfers money accordingly. First Virtual offers various types of software to allow a customer to initiate a transaction. It includes a sample Web page and a modified FTP server.

In concept, a customer must have registered with the First Virtual by providing his or her identification and credit card information. First Virtual assigns the customer an identification number. The customer browses a merchant's goods (or services) and makes the selection. The customer sends his or her First Virtual identification number to the merchant, the merchant verifies it with First Virtual clearinghouse, and First Virtual confirms it with the customer. Upon receiving confirmation, the money is transferred offline. First Virtual uses e-mail over the Internet to place and confirm orders. The transfer of money is handled offline through private networks.

Transaction Process

The process to complete a transaction on First Virtual consists of three phases: buyer registration, seller registration, and transacting a purchase.

Buyer Registration

To begin, the buyer must open an account with First Virtual. The buyer fills out a form that includes the name, address, e-mail address, and proposed passcode. The e-mail address is used to send confirmation information, and the passcode is used as part of the account name and password. Assuming that First Virtual accepts the application, First Virtual responds with a confirmation note that includes a temporary account number and a toll-free number. The buyer calls this toll-free number and inputs the temporary account number and the credit card number. Note that the credit card number is sent over the telephone network instead of the Internet. First Virtual charges the credit card number $2.00 as a new account fee.

Seller Registration

A seller first obtains a buyer's account as previously described. Next, the seller sends in a check for $10.00 that converts the buyer's account to a seller's account. First Virtual deposits the money as the new seller fee and records the seller's account number. The account number is used to deposit money electronically to the seller's account later.

Transacting a Purchase

The buyer browses the seller's goods, selects the items to purchase, and agrees to a price. The buyer then gives his or her account number to the seller.

The seller can send a transfer request to First Virtual through several ways. A simple approach is to send an e-mail message such as the following:

To: transfer@card.com
From: *seller's e-mail address*
Subject: (anything)
BUYER: *buyer's account code*
SELLER: *seller's account code*
AMOUNT: *numerical amount of money without any currency symbols*
CURRENCY: *currency id. For U.S. dollars, the currency id is "USD"*
DESCRIPTION: (A description of the purchase for later identification)

In addition, certain optional fields can be used for additional information. For example, "DELIVERY-STATUS:" can be set to "Delivered" or "Pending."

The e-mail from the seller is processed by the First Virtual clearinghouse software. Next, First Virtual sends a request for confirmation to the buyer's e-mail address. The buyer can respond with one of three responses:

YES: implies that the buyer authorizes First Virtual to bill the amount of purchase to the credit card on file.

NO: means that the buyer is refusing to permit the charges to his or her credit card. First Virtual tracks the number of occurrences of this response. If a buyer rejects the payment too often, then First Virtual might terminate the account to avoid someone taking advantage of sellers by selecting the purchase and not closing the sale.

FRAUD: entered to inform First Virtual that the purchaser never authorized the transaction. It also implies that First Virtual should investigate it as a fraud.

If the buyer authorizes the sale, then First Virtual transfers the money to the seller by charging it to the buyer's credit card. At the same time, First Virtual charges its fees to the credit card. First Virtual fees are $.29 for each transaction plus 2% of the amount of sale, according to Wayner (1996 p88).

The First Virtual scheme does not use encryption. It verifies each transaction through a centralized clearinghouse. It can stop a payment fraud when the buyer refuses to confirm the transaction. An advantage of avoiding the use of encryption is that there is no need for government approvals to distribute encryption software outside the United States. Furthermore, it avoids the need to distribute encryption software to users.

First Virtual information is also described in other references such as Lynch (1996) and Wayner (1996).

CyberCash

CyberCash started in August 1994 with the goal to work with merchants and financial institutions in providing a payment system for the Internet. It transfers information between customers, merchants, and banks using secure communications.

A customer that wants to use CyberCash services has to download the software to establish a link to CyberCash. The customer links at least one credit card to the service.

Merchants that want to use CyberCash need to establish an account with a bank that offers CyberCash to its merchants. The merchant must also modify the server software to include CyberCash's PAY button. When the customer clicks on the CyberCash PAY button, the merchant software receives information about the customer order and encrypted data containing the payment information. The merchant software verifies the data integrity of the order and the payment information, and forwards the encrypted message to CyberCash.

CyberCash client software handles various parts of commercial transactions. It establishes user identity, links credit card information to the person (customer's personal information), and keeps a log of customer transactions. It also provides the administrative and configuration services to customize and manage CyberCash software and to download new versions of client software.

The merchant server software includes installing the Cyber-Cash software and incorporating the CyberCash PAY button in the merchant's ordering pages on the Web. The merchant server also may test the changes with CyberCash before going online to handle Internet transactions.

Transaction Process

The transaction starts with the customer clicking on the PAY button. As a result, the client software sends the order information to the merchant. In addition, the client software also sends an encrypted block of payment information to the merchant.

The merchant software verifies that the payment information has not been modified. Next, the merchant software forwards the payment information to CyberCash. The merchant software also verifies that the order information has not been modified.

Upon receiving the encrypted payment information, Cyber-Cash first verifies that the payment information has not been modified during transmission. Next, CyberCash reformats the message and forwards it to the merchant's bank or to a designated credit card processing institution.

The bank or the financial institution responds to CyberCash with an approval or rejection. CyberCash forwards the status to the merchant server. The merchant server informs the customer of the results of the transaction.

Security Technologies

CyberCash provides message authentication and digital signatures using MD5 and digital signatures. For encryption, it uses a combination of DES and public keys. According to Loshin (1995), the CyberCash software has been approved for export even though it uses a strong encryption with 768-bit keys. This strong encryption is used to secure the sensitive portions of commercial transactions.

CyberCash is described in several publications including Loshin (1996), Wayner (1996), and Eastlake (1996).

Mark Twain Bank

In October 1995, the Mark Twain Bank of St. Louis, Missouri offered customers the opportunity to open accounts that could be used to withdraw or deposit electronic cash over the Internet.

A customer can obtain *ecash* (Mark Twain Bank's term for electronic cash) over the Internet by authenticating ownership of his or her account. Instead of putting the paper money in the wallet, the software stores the ecash in the hard drive. When asked to make a payment, the customer confirms the amount, purpose, and the payee. The ecash software transfers the correct value from the disk to the payee. Merchants can deposit ecash into their accounts.

The customer's computer chooses the serial numbers based on a random seed and assigns these numbers to ecash. The ecash is hidden within an encryption envelope and delivered to the bank. The bank signs the ecash and removes the originator's envelope. The ecash from the bank can be used to pay for the goods. In this way, there is no trace of the originator on the ecash.

DigiCash of Amsterdam, the Netherlands (developer of ecash) is providing the technology to Mark Twain Bank.

Details on Mark Twain Bank and DigiCash can be found in Bakel (1996), Lynch (1996), and Mark Twain (1995).

Internet Concepts

"*What is the longest distance between any Internet user and the information stored in 30,000 hosts?*"

"*an e-mail address.*"

TCP/IP Concepts

TCP/IP Background

TCP/IP is a collection of data communication protocols. These protocols allow the routing and transfer of information from one machine to another. The information may be contained in electronic mail (or e-mail), news, or various other file types.

TCP/IP has been around almost as long as UNIX. The ARPA-NET started in 1969 when the Defense Advanced Research Project Agency (DARPA) awarded a contract for the ARPA network to Bolt, Beranek, and Newman. ARPANET started growing from point-to-point leased lines to other types of communication links such as radio and satellite links. At the same time, there was a need for a common set of protocols to transfer data between different types of hosts. This need led to the inception of TCP/IP. To encourage TCP/IP usage, DARPA started providing low cost implementations of TCP/IP. The primary source for this implementation was the BSD UNIX code from the University of California at Berkeley. This implementation was developed by Bolt, Beranek and Newman Inc. (BBN) and funded by DARPA. The Berkeley implementation also offered utilities for network services. These services closely resembled the standard local services on a UNIX machine. As a result, an experienced UNIX user could quickly learn how to use the TCP/IP services. By 1983, all machines connected to the ARPANET were using TCP/IP. In addition, TCP/IP was also being implemented by many sites that were not connected to the ARPANET.

The TCP/IP protocol specifies rules that are independent of the type of machine or the underlying operating system. As a result, any vendor can implement the TCP/IP protocols on an operating system and it should interoperate with other TCP/IP implementations.

TCP/IP

TCP/IP stands for two sets of protocols: the *Transmission Control Protocol* and the *Internet Protocol*. In reality, TCP/IP consists of several protocols that collectively provide connectivity and information exchange between two hosts. These protocols can be divided into four layers, as shown in Figure A.1.

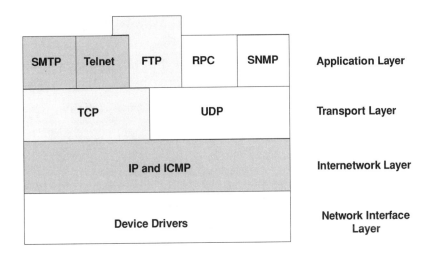

Figure A.1: TCP/IP Layers

The four layers are the Network Interface Layer, the Internetwork Layer, the Transport Layer, and the Application Layer. The *Network Interface Layer* provides the device drivers that support interactions with the communications hardware such as the Token Ring or Ethernet. The *Internetwork Layer* consists of the Internet Protocol and the Internet Control Message Protocol. The *Transport Layer* contains the Transport Control Protocol (TCP) and the User Datagram Protocol (UDP). The *Application Layer* represents the higher level protocols that are used to provide direct interface with users or applications.

Internet Protocol (IP)

The objective of *Internet Protocol (IP)* is three-fold:

- To define the format of data units for transmission over the network

- To route packets by choosing the path to transmit data through the network

- To specify protocols for unreliable, connectionless delivery

IP defines the datagram format that consists of a header and a data field. The IP header includes a source IP address and a destination IP address. Details on these addresses are provided later in this section.

IP routes packets as follows. When a packet arrives at a given node, IP checks the destination address of the packet. If the destination address is the same as that of the local node, the packet is handed over to the operating system for local processing. If the destination address is not the same as that of the local node, then IP forwards the packet based on the information in the source address and the destination address. Given the size of the Internet and the number of hosts, the routing is performed on the basis of network addresses. Once a datagram arrives in a network, it is forwarded to the appropriate host. IP maintains a routing table that consists of <N, G> pairs, where N is the network address of the destination host, and G is the IP address of the next gateway in the path towards the destination network. For a given host H, the routing table includes only those gateways that are directly connected to H. As such, each gateway must be in a network adjacent to the host H. When a datagram is to be transmitted, IP checks the destination address and extracts the network address portion (described later). Then, IP uses this network address to select the appropriate gateway from the routing table.

From the network security viewpoint, it is important to note that IP does not guarantee the validity of the source address. In fact, an attacking host can fraudulently use the source address of a legitimate host and thereby mislead the destination host. Although many operating systems ensure that the packet originating from a node contains the appropriate source address, there is no guarantee that the address has not been modified by an intermediate node in the network, or that the originating host indeed inserted the appropriate source address. This vulnerability led to a well-known Source Address Spoofing Attack, described in Chapter 1.

IP Addressing

As stated earlier, each IP packet includes a source address and a destination address. The source address and the destination address each are 32 bits long. These four bytes are often represented in a *dotted address* format. For example, the dotted address:

128.33.65.5

translates to the binary address:

10000000 00100001 01000001 00000101.

Each network address consists of three fields. The first field is the network class which is identified by the first few bits of the address. The second field provides the network identifier within the network class. The third field contains the host address within the identified network.

Network Class	High Order Bits	Network Address	Host Address
A	0 1 bit	0-127 7 bits	0-16,777,214 24 bits
B	10 2 bits	0-16364 14 bits	0-65,534 16 bits
C	110 3 bits	0-2,097,152 21 bits	0-254 8 bits
D	1111 4 bits	multicast address 28 bits	

Table A.1: IP Address Format

Class A Addresses

Class A addresses are used for large networks that have more than 2^{16} hosts. A class A address is identified by the leftmost bit of the address field set to 0. The next 7 bits include the network address. So only 128 networks are allowed in this class. However, each network in this class can have 2^{24} or approximately 16 million hosts in each network.

Class B Addresses

A *class B address* is used for networks that have between 2^8 to 2^{16} hosts. In a class B address, the two leftmost bits are set to *10*. The network address is provided in the next 14 bits. The remaining 16 bits are used for the host address, so each network can have 2^{16} or approximately 65,000 hosts. This network class is very popular since a class C network can consist of no more than 254 hosts. At the same time, class B can have only 2^{14} or 16,364 networks. Consequently, this class is running out of available network addresses.

Class C Addresses

For a class C address, the leftmost three bits are set to *110*. The network address is provided in the next 21 bits, followed by 8 bits for host address. As such, approximately 2 million networks are permitted in this class. However, only 254 hosts can be in a given class C network.

Class D Addresses

The class D addresses are reserved for broadcasting to several machines that conform to the same protocol.

Internet Control Message Protocol (ICMP)

Internet Control Message Protocol (ICMP) provides for a gateway to report error conditions to the originating source. A *gateway* is a host that interconnects two networks. ICMP provides for reporting error conditions and in some cases suggests possible actions. However, ICMP does not make IP more reliable. ICMP is considered an integral part of IP and must be implemented by each IP module. ICMP does not report errors on ICMP packets to avoid infinite repetitions.

Sockets

A *socket* or *socket address* consists of the IP address and port number for the higher level application or protocol that should receive the packet. This address is usually written as the pair: <IP Address, port number>. The IP address identifies the address of the host on the network. The port number is a 16-bit field that specifies which application or protocol should receive the packet. For some of the commonly used applications, specific port numbers have been assigned. For example, the port number for Telnet is 23, SMTP is 25, FTP is 20 for data and 21 for control. Figure A.2 depicts the way socket address is used by a TCP/IP host.

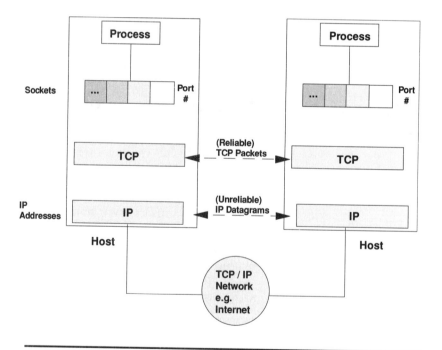

Figure A.2: Socket Usage

User Datagram Protocol (UDP)

User Datagram Protocol (UDP) is a connectionless protocol that resides in the transport layer, as shown in Figure A.1. UDP allows for basic message exchange without any overhead for flow control, reliability, or error recovery. UDP simply multiplexes and demultiplexes packets so the application can send or receive a complete message, whereas the IP layer receives or delivers data units in terms of packets. If an application requires assurance that the message is delivered, or that the packet is delivered error-free, then TCP should be used. For real-time traffic, a UDP connection reduces the response time by avoiding the overhead of TCP. As such, UDP is often used by inquiry/response applications where small data units are exchanged and the traffic is real time.

Transport Control Protocol (TCP)

Transport Control Protocol (TCP) describes a protocol for reliable and error- free transfer of messages between applications. TCP has the ability to recover from transmission errors so that fragmented packets can be reassembled in proper sequence. It provides a virtual connection to user processes or applications. This connection is called a *virtual circuit* and is uniquely identified by the quadruple:

<localhost, localport, remotehost, remoteport>.

TCP provides a reliable transmission among two hosts through the use of a data and acknowledgement protocol. Each packet is acknowledged by the receiver. To overlap, the sender can send more than one packet without receiving the acknowledgements. This scheme is called *sliding window protocol*. If the sender has not received an acknowledgement for its last k packets, then it stops transmission of additional packets. Here, k is the window size for this connection. TCP supports the sliding window protocol by allowing the window size to vary over time. The window size is increased or decreased based on the availability of free buffers at the receiving host. Details on sliding window protocol can be found in Comer (1991) and Ahuja (1982).

The acknowledgement protocol also ensures error-free delivery of packets and recovery from lost packets. As stated earlier, the receiver acknowledges each packet. The acknowledgement specifies whether the data was received with or without error. The sender also maintains a timer that starts when the packet is transmitted. If an acknowledgement is not received within a predicted time period, TCP assumes that the packet is lost and retransmits the packet. Given that the TCP connection is between two endpoints, the connection may traverse one or more high-speed or low-speed links. So, the value of timeout for retransmission may vary depending on the underlying transmission links. This problem is addressed by TCP monitoring the performance of each connection and deriving estimated values for timeouts.

The Internet uses TCP/IP for its underlying networking protocols. Besides the TCP/IP protocols, the Internet consists of several services that we will describe in the next section.

Internet Services

During the past few years, the Internet was rediscovered. Although the Internet's origins go back to 1969, it was not until the mid-1990s that the Internet swept our society with a revolution. We discussed the history of the Internet in the *Introduction*. Extend your imagination to a network of millions of interconnected users who can communicate with each other as well as access information and services at tens of thousands of hosts across the world, and you get a glimpse of the potential of the Internet.

The Internet is to information what the telephone network is to voice conversations. The telephone network does not consist of any information, it simply provides the means to communicate as long as the attaching telephones conform to certain well-defined standards. Similarly, the Internet does not contain any data, but provides access to data for users. The Internet specifies standards for users or data hosts to attach to it. Another similarity between the telephone network and the Internet is that a world-wide organization does not exist that manages and controls these networks. The Internet components conform to a collection of standards that are specified by a group of organizations. The Internet Architecture Board (IAB) provides oversight to the Internet Engineering Task Force (IETF). IETF is responsible for defining and approving the protocols for the Internet. There are other associated organizations for related services such as the Internet Assigned Number Authority, the Federal Networking Council, and the Center for Emergency Response Team (CERT).

Once connected to the Internet, a user or a host has access to a variety of information and services. These services are provided through applications or user processes that use the TCP/IP protocols. In the following, we review some of the commonly used services:

- Electronic Mail
- TELNET
- File Transfer Protocol (FTP)
- Mailing Lists

- Usenet Newsgroups

- Archie

- Gopher

- Veronica

We have not included the World Wide Web here, which is addressed in detail in Appendix B. Before describing the electronic mail service of the Internet, we must introduce the concept of a domain name system.

Domain Name System

The dotted addresses of the Internet are cumbersome to remember and enter. To make life easy, the Internet provides facilities to use symbolic names instead of dotted addresses. The *Domain Name System* allows the use of symbolic names instead of dotted addresses. For example, you could enter

   telnet company.com

instead of entering the dotted address

   telnet 112.3.8.25.

The symbolic names are assigned using a *domain name hierarchy.* The hierarchy starts with the highest name being the domain name. Some of the common domain names are listed in Table A.2

Domain Name	Description
edu	Educational Institution
gov	Government Institution
com	Commercial Organization
mil	Military Group

Table A.2: Domain Name Hierarchy

For example, consider a hypothetical company, *MYCOMPANY Inc*, on the Internet. Its domain name would quite likely be mycompany.com. A user of the company can be associated with its domain. For example, in this hypothetical company John Smith may have the address *johnsmith @ mycompany.com.*

Finally, a **name server** provides the translation from symbolic names to dotted IP addresses. A name server is installed for each leaf of the domain name hierarchy tree.

Electronic Mail

Electronic mail (or *E-mail*) allows transmission and delivery of messages, notes, or memos between Internet users. E-mail is provided by the Internet as well as various online services, such as *CompuServe, Prodigy,* etc. The following description addresses the e-mail service on the Internet.

E-mail consists of two parts, the address portion and the message text. The address portion consists of several lines that have specific meanings. The line beginning with *To:* contains the e-mail address of the intended recipient. The *From:* line includes the e-mail address of the sender of the mail. The *Reply To:* line is optional and provides the e-mail address to be used for sending a reply. If the *Reply To:* line is not present, then the *From:* line is used to determine the address for sending the reply.

E-mail often uses the symbolic addresses. An e-mail address consists of two parts: *local-port @ domain-name*. For example, my e-mail address at IBM is *vahuja @ vnet.ibm.com*.

TELNET

TELNET provides the capability to log on a remote host. It requires a TELNET client at the user's machine and a TELNET server in the remote host. When a user initiates the TELNET program, the TELNET client communicates the request to the TELNET server at the remote host. In effect, the TELNET client transfers each key stroke to the TELNET server. The TELNET server delivers the commands from the TELNET client to the local host. The TELNET server also sends all the responses from the local host to the TELNET client. In this way, the TEL-NET server at the remote host acts on behalf of the TELNET client, as shown in Figure A.3. Note that to the remote host, the user appears as if he or she is locally logged on to the host.

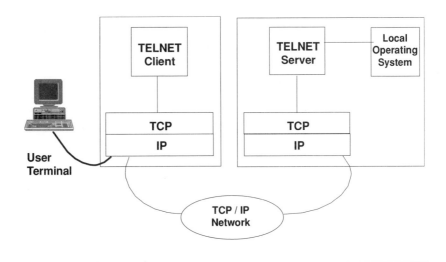

Figure A.3: TELNET Client and Server in TCP/IP Network

TELNET is one of the most commonly used applications on the Internet. It is frequently used to access remote hosts to search the directories for files. Once the file is located, then FTP is used to transfer the file.

File Transfer Protocol (FTP)

File Transfer Protocol (FTP) provides the transfer of files between two TCP/IP hosts. An FTP client can request a file from the host where the FTP server resides. FTP also allows for an FTP client to transfer a file from the FTP client host to the FTP server host, as shown in Figure A.4. For reliability purposes, FTP uses TCP protocols.

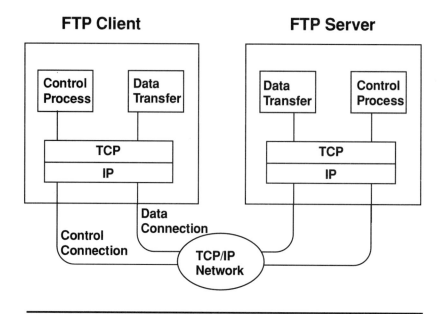

Figure A.4: FTP Client/Server

FTP provides some distinct facilities to users. First, FTP offers an interactive session that lets you search and select the files for transfer. For example, you can look at a remote directory, search the desired file, and request for a transfer. Secondly, you can also specify the file format such as EBCDIC or ASCII. Finally, FTP also allows user authentication by requiring you to enter your ID and the password.

FTP is also one of the most commonly used applications on the Internet. FTP is mostly used to provide *anonymous* FTP. *Anonymous FTP* lets any user access an FTP site. The user name is *anonymous*. The password is often your e-mail address in the form of *user @ host*. Once you are logged on, you can enter commands for the FTP client. The *GET* command is entered to receive a file from the FTP server, and the *PUT* command is used to send a file to the FTP server host.

The FTP server receives the FTP requests from the client to set up an FTP connection called the *control connection*. As a result, the FTP server initiates a new process to handle the specific control connection. This new process handles the control connection from the client, but sets up another process for the *data transfer connection*. The data transfer connection transfers the file between the client and the server.

FTP is available at sites where even TELNET is not available. In the last few years, user friendly versions of FTP have been developed and marketed. In these programs, the user simply has to click on the selections to start an FTP session and to transfer the files. When used in conjunction with Archie (described later), it will even search the file for you.

Mailing Lists

The Internet *mailing list* is similar to the mailing lists used for postal mail. By enlisting your e-mail address in a mailing list, you will start receiving all the e-mail sent to that mailing list. There are tens of thousands of mailing lists on the Internet and you can easily be swamped by the e-mail overload.

To subscribe to a mailing list through a list server, you send an e-mail to the *listserv* program. Inside the e-mail message text, you may be asked to include words such as:

subscribe securityfans Vijay Ahuja

The listserv program reads this text and includes my name in the hypothetical list called *securityfans* by including my e-mail address in the mailing list. After some time, I will get a message that confirms my enrollment.

Once you are listed in a mailing list, you automatically receive a copy of any message posted to that list. Sometimes, the title of the list may not be sufficient to understand the details of the topic being considered or the type of conversations underway on that topic.

Usenet Newsgroups

Usenet is a collection of computers and users that are interconnected over the Internet. *Usenet newsgroups* are groups established by people that share a common interest. Although similar in concept to the mailing lists, there are several differences between mailing lists and newsgroups:

- Although mailing lists are accessible through e-mail, newsgroups require full Internet accounts. As a result, there are 30+ million users that can access mailing lists, but only about a third of them have access to newsgroups.

- Although mailing lists provide instant distribution, Usenet machines store the messages sent by the users and periodically forward them to other Usenet machines. In order to access and retrieve messages of your desired newsgroup, you need a *news reader*. The news reader program selectively retrieves the news and messages you desire.

Usenet newsgroups change over time. New newsgroups are added all the time. An existing newsgroup may be split if there is too much traffic, or dissolved if there is a lack of interest. There is no enforcement body and changes to the newsgroups are made within some commonly accepted conventions.

Seven major newsgroup categories constitute the top level of the newsgroup hierarchy, as shown in Table A.3. For each category, there are several, sometimes hundreds, of sub-newsgroups.

Category	Description
ALT	Alternate topics that are not covered in other categories.
COMP	Computer related topics
MISC	Miscellaneous topics of interest
NEWS	News
REC	Topics related to recreation
SCI	Topics on sciences
SOC	Social topics
TALK	Topics similar to talk-radio

Table A.3: Newsgroup Categories

The name of a newsgroup identifies the general area of the topic. A very broad variety of newsgroup topics are included, for example *alt.elvis.king*, *rec.roller-coaster*, and *soc.culture.sri-lanka*. The administrator of a Usenet computer can decide which newsgroups will be made available to the local users.

Archie

Archie provides the user with the capability to search for files on the Internet. Archie uses the same client/server concept as other Internet services. Most Internet hosts have an Archie client that you can access simply by entering the word *archie*. The Archie client accesses an Archie server. The Archie servers contain lists of files on the Internet. You can request to search for a given word or text string. The Archie server responds with a list of hosts that contain files that include the text string in the filename.

For example, you can enter the command *archie sec*. The archie client sends this command to the archie server. The archie server looks for all the files that include the words sec in the filenames, and returns the following information for the selected files:

- The host names
- For each identified host, the directory in which the file resides in that host
- The exact filename

You can then use the *anonymous FTP* to retrieve the desired files.

Archie is particularly useful when you are looking for a particular filename. If you know only the topic and not the filename, then you should use Gopher, described next.

Gopher

Gopher was designed in 1991 by computer users at the University of Minnesota. *Gopher* is a convenient way to access information on topics of interest. In contrast to Archie, Gopher does not use the filename approach in searching for files.

A Gopher client must be available at the user host system. The University of Minnesota has widely distributed the Gopher client code. Once you access a Gopher server, you can select the type of information you need. You can also access other Gopher servers on the Internet.

Gopher works as follows. Suppose that General Motors wants to provide information about its cars. So, General Motors creates a Gopher server and stores information about its cars. On accessing this hypothetical Gopher server for GM, you would get a menu that displays the types of General Motors cars. First, select the car type followed by a selection of the desired car model. Next, you can choose the type of desired information for the selected car model.

Consider another example. I want to access information about the airfare from New York to Dallas. Let us assume that Eastern Airlines has created a Gopher server. So, this hypothetical Gopher server, *gopher.eastern.com*, contains information about the travel cities and the airfare. Assuming I have a Gopher client code, I enter *gopher gopher.eastern.com*. In response, the Eastern Gopher server presents the From/To city combinations. I can select the desired combination for New York/Dallas and find information on flights and airfares for those flights.

Gopher *subject trees* are lists of resources classified by categories. You start the search with a subject tree that covers the area of interest.

As we will describe in Appendix B, the World Wide Web approach is built around similar concepts. So, over the last few years, many of the Gopher sites have been converted to Web sites.

Veronica

Veronica is similar to Archie in functions. Whereas Archie searches the filenames for a given text string, Veronica searches the Gopher menu items at different Gopher servers. Most Gopher servers have Veronica search facilities built in the Gopher services. So, if you browse Gopher for some time you may come across some items such as *Veronica Search*. Once you select that item, you are prompted to enter a search term using Veronica.

Veronica servers search Gopher servers at night to update the Veronica database with all the new menu items it finds.

The topics of TCP/IP and Internet services are included in various books. There are books on TCP/IP, such as (Comer 1991). There are books (Mathiesen 1995, Ellsworth 1994, Cheswick 1994, Kantor 1995) on various aspects of Internet or the Web that also include a review of the Internet services.

World Wide Web

"What made the Internet? The World Wide Web.
What made the Web? Graphics.
What will make your Web site really hot? Graphics—good, relevant graphics."

David P. Busch, "In this World—Image is Everything."
NetGuide. March 1996. p. 56.

The World Wide Web, or simply *the Web*, is a collection of interconnected hosts that provide easy user access to stored information. The Web has swept the Internet community and pushed the Internet to tens of thousands of new homes and businesses. This revolution, that some call *Webolution* (Wiggins 1995), is spreading at a phenomenal rate.

The Web is based on the client/server paradigm. A *Web browser*, also called a *browser*, *Web client*, or a *client*, accesses a Web server. The Web browser provides access through easy-to-use interfaces. The *Web server* stores and serves documents that are defined in a special language called the *HyperText Markup Language (HTML)*. The HTML documents may be linked to other HTML documents stored on the Internet. Through the use of such linkages among HTML documents, the Web permits easy access to information dispersed across the Internet. The applications can access the HTML data through a *Common Gateway Interface (CGI)*. These components of a Web network are shown in Figure B.1. The Web browser communicates with the Web server over a transfer protocol called *HyperText Transfer Protocol (HTTP)*. HTTP runs over TCP/IP as shown in Figure B.1.

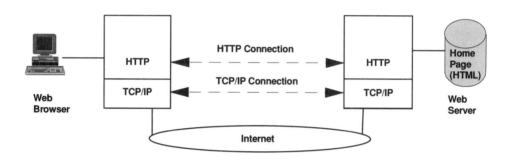

Figure B.1: Web Connection

We will begin this appendix with a review of the background of the Web. Then we will focus on the three fundamental elements of the Web, namely the HTTP, the HTML, and the CGI.

Web Background

Although the Web only started gaining popularity around 1993, the underlying concepts for the Web have been around for quite sometime. Web documents use *hyperlinks* to link Web documents to data repositories located elsewhere on the Internet. A hyperlink provides connection from one page on the Web to another page. The term *hypertext* relates to documents that include hyperlinks. This approach of linked documents has been around for several years. The following overview uses Wiggins (1995) and Kantor (1995); both are good references for details on the Web.

Ted Nelson, a computing visionary, published a book in 1981 called *Literary Machines* (Southbend, Indiana, 1981 from Wiggins 1995). In this book, he described a system called *Xanadu* that allowed readers to create hypertext consisting of linked nodes.

The roots of today's World Wide Web can be traced to Tim Berners-Lee. He conceived of a hypertext tool in the early 1980s and developed it for his own use. While employed at CERN (the European Particle Physics Institute) in Geneva, Switzerland, Berners-Lee started thinking of ways in which a hypertext project could help the high-energy physics community at CERN and around the world. In March 1989, he proposed a hypertext project.

Berners-Lee and his colleague Robert Cailliau coauthored a document on hypertext in November 1990. This document presents their views on hypertext. As quoted in Wiggins (1995), the document states that hypertext is a way to link and access information of various kinds as a web of nodes in which the user can browse at will. The document also states that hypertext potentially provides a single user-interface to many large classes of stored information such as reports, notes, databases, computer documentation, and online system help. The documents are linked in such a way that the user can go from one document to another to find the desired information. The network of links is called *the Web*.

Berners-Lee got funding for his project and the World Wide Web was released for use at CERN in May 1991. In addition, CERN introduced several Web tools by August 1991. Berners-Lee presented the World Wide Web at a session at the Hypertext '91 conference in San Antonio, Texas. In January 1992, the line-mode browser was made available for anonymous FTP. By July 1992, CERN announced a library of World Wide Web tools. These tools are still used as a source of reference for developing Web browser and server software.

Another well-known browser was developed by the National Center for Supercomputing Applications (NCSA) at the University of Illinois in Urbana-Champaign, Illinois. It was developed by a student, Marc Andreesen (who later started Netscape) along with Eric Bina, a programmer at NCSA. In February 1993, Andreesen announced the *Mosaic*, an X/Windows Web browser.

Since 1993, there have been numerous additions to the Web browsers and servers. Various computer vendors, including IBM and Netscape have introduced Web-related products. At the same time, several new technologies are emerging that enhance the services and facilities for users and applications on the web.

HyperText Transfer Protocol (HTTP)

HTTP was born in CERN along with other elements of the World Wide Web. HTTP is a light-weight protocol that provides communications between the Web browsers and the servers. HTTP was developed as a stateless protocol and is conceptually simple. You begin by entering a URL (described later) or clicking on a hyperlink. As a result, the client establishes a connection with the server. Once connected, the client sends a request to the server. The server executes the request, returns a response, and closes the connection.

The original version of HTTP is referred to as HTTP/0.9. It was later replaced by HTTP/1.0. HTTP/1.0 consisted of a discussion by several people on *www-talk* including Tim Berners-Lee and Ari Luotonen. As of this writing, HTTP/1.0 Internet Draft 05 (Berners-Lee 1996) is available on the Internet. We use this Internet draft in this section, and it should be treated as work in progress.

Before describing details of HTTP flow, we must define some concepts.

Uniform Resource Locator (URL)

A *Uniform Resource Locator (URL)* identifies the location of an item on the Web. It consists of the protocol followed by the fully-qualified host name. It may also include the path and the filename. For example, the URL for CommerceNet is *http:// www.commerce.net*.

Universal Resource Identifier (URI)

The HTTP command begins with a **Universal Resource Identifier (URI)**. URIs have also been known as **WWW addresses**, **Uniform Document Identifiers**, and a combination of URL and names (URNs). For the purposes of HTTP, URIs are formatted strings that identify a network resource via name, location, or any other characteristic. A URL is a form of a URI. Details of URI formats are provided in Berners-Lee (1996).

Multipurpose Internet Mail Extensions (MIME)

The *MIME* protocol specifies how information can be included in the Internet mail exchange in other than standard ASCII text.

The HTTP protocol uses a request/response paradigm. First, a client establishes a connection with a server. Then, she or he sends a request to the server. The request consists of an identification of the request method, a Universal Resource Identifier, protocol version, request modifiers, client information, and possibly the body content. The server response consists of a status line that includes the message's protocol version, a success or error code, a message containing server information, body content, and some other information.

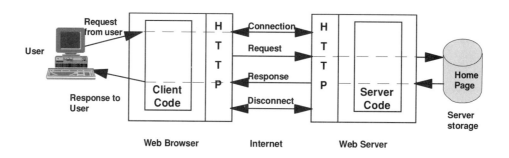

Figure B.2: HTTP Flow

Figure B.2 illustrates the sequence of events that take place to access a home page. We will access a home page of a hypothetical company called *mycompany* at *http://www.mycompany.com*. This is the Uniform Resource Locator (URL) of *mycompany's* home page.

The sequence begins with you clicking on the URL address *http://www.mycompany.com*. As a result, the Web client code initiates a request for a TCP/IP connection with the IP address for that URL. Once a connection is established, an HTTP command is sent to the server.

The HTTP server response begins with a response code and a message. For example, the response may read *HTTP/1.0 200 OK*. While browsing on the Internet, you may see some of these codes. For example, I have often seen the 404 status code displayed when the target resource cannot be found. A list of the status codes is tabulated below. Additional details are available in Berners-Lee (1996, Section 9).

200	OK
201	Created
202	Accepted
204	No Content
301	Moved Permanently
302	Moved Temporarily
304	Not Modified
400	Bad Request
401	Unauthorized
403	Forbidden
404	Not Found
500	Internal Server Error
501	Not Implemented
502	Bad Gateway
503	Service Unavailable

Table B.1: HTTP Status Codes

Source: T. Berners-Lee, R. Fielding, H. Frystyk, "Hypertext Transfer Protocol - HTTP/1.0," Internet Draft - Work in Progress. February 19,1996. Section 6.1.1.

The server can also attach other types of optional information. For example, the Content-Type header provides the type of data being sent to the client. This information helps the client code possibly to launch another application that can display the data received from the server. After the response is completely transmitted, the server closes the connection.

If it is graphical data, then the request/response sequence would be repeated for each image until the complete page was transmitted.

Method

The *method* specifies the actions to be performed on the resource. It is included in the request from the client. Three types of methods are permitted; GET, HEAD, and POST.

GET

The *GET* method retrieves whatever information is identified in the requested URI. A conditional GET method may specify that the identified resource be transferred only if it has been modified since the date included in the request.

HEAD

The *HEAD* method is similar to the GET method except that no entity body[*] is included in the response from the server. The

---

[*] A request/response message may transfer an entity within the message. An *entity* consists of an entity header and an entity body. The entity header defines the format of the entity body such as the content encoding and content type. Complete details are provided in Berners-Lee (1996, Section 7.0).

header information in response to a HEAD request should be identical to the header information in response to a GET request.

POST

The *POST* method requests that the server accept the entity enclosed in the request as a new subordinate of the resource identified in URI. The posted entity will be subordinate to the target URI in the same way as a file is subordinate to a directory, or a news item is subordinate to a newsgroup.

To minimize the overhead, HTTP is a stateless protocol. As such, each request/response interaction is independent of any other interaction between the same client and server. Consequently, there is limited information available to describe user behavior. The usual measure for client behavior is simply the number of hits, which is the number of HTTP requests.

Security for HTTP

HTTP lacks privacy since the protocol does not employ any encryption. However, HTTP includes an authentication scheme for protected files. The protected files require authentication information to be included in the request from the client. If a file is protected and the client does not include authentication information in the request, then the server returns an error to the client. Most browsers that support authentication also include the intelligence to reuse the authentication information of a given user. In this way, a client may not be required to enter authentication information more than once[*] during a ses-

---

[*] There are several benefits in reusing user's authentication information during a session. The topic of secure single logon is addressed in details in Ahuja (1996).

sion on the Web. However, the *basic* authentication scheme transmits the passwords as plain text, encoded but not encrypted.

HTTP 1.1 can be extended with custom extensions such as extended HTTP behavior by adding new message headers. Protocol Extension Protocol (PEP) (Khare 1996) includes features for standardizing scope, strength, and ordering of such extensions. PEP also includes an extensible negotiation framework. This document reflects work in progress.

Finally, to enhance security for HTTP exchanges, two security schemes have been developed: *Secure HyperText Transfer Protocol (SHTTP)* and *Secure Sockets Layer (SSL)*. These schemes are described in Chapter 6.

HyperText Markup Language (HTML)

HyperText Markup Language (HTML) is a simple authoring language that is used to create hypertext documents. HTML has been used in the Web since 1990. HTML 2.0 is documented in RFC 1866 (Berners-Lee 1995) and roughly corresponds to the HTML capabilities in common use prior to June 1994. As of this writing, HTML 3 (Ragett 1996) is a working draft that provides the HTML Table Model to be used for different types of tables.

HTML is a document type described in *Standard Generalized Markup Language (SGML)*. SGML formalizes the structure of documents and provides the capability of these documents to be interchanged among different document processing packages. HTML 2.0 version is defined as *SGML document type definition (DTD)*. As a result, the definition of a document as an HTML document is based on its conformance to SGML definition.

HTML documents are portable from one platform to another. When you create a page with HTML, you do not define the fonts for the text. HTML specifies generic sizes for the text along with formatting rules. Each browser uses the HTML elements (such as anchors and tags described later) to determine how to process and display the text. As such, the same HTML text can be processed by different browsers.

HTML documents consist of plain text along with several markup directives called *tags*. There may also be one or more URLs of other documents linked to an HTML document.

Structurally, the HTML document consists of a head and a body. The head includes information about the document such as its title. The text of the document is included in the body of the document.

HTML Tags

Here, we will review some of the important tags for HTML 2.0; complete details can be found in Berners-Lee (1995). *Tags* are strings of characters enclosed in angle brackets and represent instructions to the browser software on how to display the text. Tags usually come in pairs and are enclosed within angle brackets. A given pair of tags encompasses a specific action. Tags are case insensitive. For example, the tags for title can be written as *<TITLE>*, or *<title>*.

The first pair of tags informs the browser software that this is an HTML document. *<HTML>* specifies the beginning of the document, and *</HTML>* specifies the end of the HTML document. For some browsers, the *<HTML>* and *</HTML>* tags are not required.

HEAD

A pair of tags are specified to identify the Head portion of the document. It begins with *<HEAD>* and ends with *</HEAD>*.

TITLE

Every HTML document must include a pair of tags for its title. The title should represent the document contents in a global sense. For example, a title such as *Introduction* for this section is quite meaningless without other information. Instead, it would be preferable to call this section *Introduction to HTML Tags.*

The tags for title are specified in a pair, *<TITLE>* and *</TITLE>*.

Example: *<TITLE>* Introduction to HTML *</TITLE>*.

The head portion of the document may also include other information such as hyperlinks.

BODY

The body of the document is delineated between the tag pair *<BODY>* and *</BODY>*.

The complete text of the document is included within this tag pair. This tag pair is optional; many browsers do not require this tag pair.

Heading Tags

HTML allows six levels of heading tags. The largest and boldest size header is encapsulated between *<H1>* and *</H1>*. The next smaller and lighter header is *<H2>* and *</H2>*, next is *<H3>* and *</H3>*, and so on. The exact size and boldness of each header is determined by the browser's local configuration. To make the document text more readable, more than one size header should be used.

Paragraph and Line Break

You can use the *<p>* start a paragraph. If, instead of a new paragraph, you simply want to start a new line, then you should use the line break tag **
**. The *<p>* and *
* tags do not require the corresponding ending tags *</P>* and *</BR>*.

The following example shows a complete HTML document for a home page of this appendix.

```
<html>
<title>Book on Secure Commerce</title>
<h1> Secure Commerce on the Internet </h1>
<h2> Appendix B: World Wide Web </h2>
This Appendix presents the concepts and approaches that constitute
the World Wide Web. The World Wide Web uses HTML to define the
documents, HTTP to communicate between the browser and server,
and CGI to permit the server to interface with applications.
</html>
```

Hyperlinks

A hypertext link, or *hyperlink*, is a pointer from a place in a document to another destination. In the simplest form, the destination may be another document although it could be an image or another form of object. A hypertext link is specified through the use of a pair of *anchor* tags. This tag pair, *<A>* and *</A>*, provides the specification of the destination. Anchor tags also permit specification of certain tag attributes. An anchor tag must include one or both of the NAME and HREF attributes. Consider the following example.

> *<A HREF="company-url">company information</A>*

Here, the <A starts the anchor tag and it includes the HREF attribute. The HREF attribute indicates that this anchor is the start of a hypertext link and that the URL for the destination is the value of the attribute. The </A> tag specifies the end of the anchor tag. The browser software highlights the text between the <A> and the </A> tags. So for this example, the text *company information* is highlighted. The NAME attribute specifies that the anchor is the destination of a link that has been established elsewhere.

Additional details on the hypertext links can be found in Berners-Lee (1995) and Ford (1995).

Images

HTML allows use of inline images in a document. To include an *image*, the **IMG** element is used as follows:

> *<IMG SRC="img-url" [ALT="description"] [ALIGN="specify"]>*

The image element begins with <IMG, followed by some attributes. The image element does not require the end tag </IMG>. This end tag is illegal and may lead to some undesirable results with some browsers. The SRC attribute must be included; it specifies the URL of the image file. The ALT attribute provides the alternative of the textual description of the image. For text-mode browsers, this description can be displayed instead of the image. All other attributes are considered optional.

The default alignment of an image is with the baseline of the text invoking the image file. This can be overridden by using the ALIGN attribute. The *ALIGN* attribute can specify the alignment to be TOP, MIDDLE, or BOTTOM. For example, if the ALIGN attribute specifies TOP, then the image is aligned such that the top of the image is in line with the text.

Image Creation

Images can be created using software tools, drawings, CAD (Computer Aided Design), or other graphics packages. Images can also be created from fax modems, scanners, and digital cameras. In addition, photographic negatives or transparencies can also be converted to images. The most common graphics file format is *GIF*. It was devised by CompuServe Inc. and is supported by many browsers. New browsers also support the display of images in other formats such as *JPEG*.

GIF is based on an eight-bit format that allows a display of 256 distinct colors. *JPEG* is a 24-bit format that gives a total of 16 million colors. To display so many colors, you also need a corresponding capability on the workstation. Low-end PCs have a palette of four, sixteen, or 256 colors. Furthermore, these colors also have to be shared with other applications running concurrently. JPEG also allows variable image compression. As a result, a JPEG file may be a half or a third of the size of a corresponding GIF file. However, the compression leads to degradation in the quality of the compressed image.

Several enhancements can be designed for images. One such enhancement is the *image map* that allows different effects by clicking on different parts of an image. For example, by clicking on a particular city, you can view pertinent details of that city.

Development Tools

To develop an HTML document, several software tools may be utilized. HTML editors can provide features that are often available in word processing software: spelling checkers, thesauruses, and so on. It is quite possible that a perfectly valid HTML document may be developed without the use of any editors or other tools. The HTML tags are mostly simple and straightforward, although additional effort may be required to create graphical images.

According to Ford (1995), a number of tools are available that can validate the syntax of HTML documents. These tools can be used to ensure that appropriate syntax rules have been followed in the HTML document. In addition, services are available on the Web to validate an HTML document and to provide answers to short questions about HTML syntax.

Web Server

At the web server, there are three capabilities that collectively provide a wide variety of services for users and applications. First, there is the *Common Gateway Interface (CGI)* between the applications and the server. Next, there are the programs that use CGI. These programs are called *CGI scripts*. Finally, there are the *forms* that are presented to the user for providing input. Before describing the forms and scripts, we must review the concept and elements of the Common Gateway Interface (CGI).

Common Gateway Interface (CGI)

Consider the problem when a client requests certain information that is not already stored in the server as an HTML document. To satisfy such a request, the web server requires a
program that dynamically will generate an HTML document.
These documents are called *dynamic documents*. This capability permits documents to be generated *on the fly* from information that may be derived from the input by the client. The
server code interfaces with the software to generate dynamic
documents. This interface is called *Common Gateway Inter-*
face (CGI), and the programs that generate the dynamic documents are called CGI scripts. This is shown in Figure B.3. The
client may provide certain input through a form to be filled out
by the user, as we will explain later.

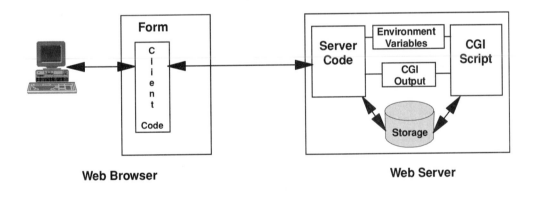

Figure B.3: CGI Usage

A typical scenario using CGI may work as follows:

1. The user fills out a *form* at the browser screen.
   It includes a request that a CGI script be run by the
   server.

2. The server retrieves the appropriate CGI script information and identifies the CGI script. The server also obtains information from the forms and provides it to the CGI script through environment variables.

3. The CGI script is executed and the results are provided to the server. The server delivers the data to the client, and the client in turn displays it to the user.

CGI Input: Command-Line Arguments

A client can request for the execution of a CGI script as follows. The author of an HTML document inserts the name of the CGI script as an attribute in the anchor tag. When the user clicks on the text included in the anchor tag, the browser sends a request to the server to execute the indicated program. The tag line may appear as follows.

<A HREF="cgi-mycode.exe">Click to run my code.</A>

Besides the program name, the client may need to send some parameters or other information to the CGI program. The client can send information to the server through two types of command-line options: *query string* and *extra path*.

In a query string, the client includes the information in the anchor tag line by separating it with a question mark (?). For example, if the client wants to send a set of parameters, then it is included in the query string as shown.

<A HREF="cgi-mycode.exe?parameters">

In an extra path, the information is included by adding one or more slashes (/) after the program name. For example:

<A HREF="cgi-mycode.exe/parameters">

CGI Input: Environment Variables

The server receives the information from the client and forwards it to the CGI scripts as part of the environment variables. There are several environment variables that are useful in communicating with the CGI programs; some of them are described next.

CONTENT_TYPE: This variable identifies the MIME type of data. It is set when there is data attached to the request and is passed as standard input stream to the CGI program.

CONTENT_LENGTH: If the data is attached as standard input stream, then its length is included in this variable.

GATEWAY_INTERFACE: The CGI version is specified in this variable. It is included as the *name/version*. For example, CGI Version 1.1 is specified as CGI/1.1.

REMOTE_ADDR: This variable identifies the Internet address of the host that originated the request.

REMOTE_HOST: If available, the name of the requesting host is included here.

AUTH_TYPE: If the script is protected, then this variable includes the type of authentication method used.

REMOTE_USER: The name of the authenticated user is included in this variable. This variable applies only if the script is protected and user authentication is supported.

CGI Output

The CGI output may simply point to a specific location such as a url address. In this case, the CGI script is telling the server to inform the client to redirect the request to a specific URL address. If the document addressed by the URL is located at the server, then the server usually intercepts the response, handles the redirection, and delivers the document to the client. The response information is contained as part of HTTP headers. The environment variable CONTENT_TYPE is included to inform the browser how to interpret the data from the CGI scripts.

CGI Scripts

CGI scripts can be written in any language that is supported by the server. For UNIX servers, it is common to use shell or Perl. A simple example of a CGI script written in Bourne shell is shown below. This script displays the date as retrieved from the date command on the system.

A sample CGI Script follows.

```
echo "content-Type: text/html"
echo
echo "<HEAD><TITLE>Date-Time Information</TITLE><HEAD>"
echo "<BODY>"
echo "The current date and time is:"
   date
   echo "</BODY>"
```

Figure B.4: A Simple CGI Script that Returns the Date

There are several useful CGI scripts and tools written in Perl and available on the Internet. For existing applications, CGI scripts are written as *wrappers*. The wrapper transforms the information from CGI inputs to a format appropriate for the existing application. It also converts the output of the existing application into an HTML document along with appropriate header information.

Script Identification

CGI scripts are stored in special directories that are identified in the server's configuration files. The CGI script must also be stored in a format such that it is executable. So for MS-DOS, the script must include the extension .EXE or .COM. For UNIX systems, use the *chmod* command to set the execute bit to on for the CGI scripts.

There are several utility programs also available to help in writing scripts. Details on HTML and CGI scripts can found in several books such as Ford (1995), LeVitus (1996b), and Morrison (1995).

Forms

HTML provides a facility for users to provide input by filling out forms. *Forms* require HTML documents that solicit input from the user and the software in the server to process the input from the forms. When the user submits the form, the contents of the data are transmitted to the server.

Forms can be used in several ways. For example, a university may solicit information from applicants for admission through forms. On receipt of the information, the server CGI scripts provide a *thank you* graphic to the applicant, and the admissions system processes the application.

The form element can be specified through a pair of *FORM* tags, as follows:

<FORM [ACTION="url-address"] [METHOD="selected-method"]
[ENCTYPE="selected-encoding"]
definitions of fields
</FORM>

Each attribute of the FORM element is optional.

The ACTION attribute specifies the URL address of the script to process this form. Default value is the URL address of the document.

The METHOD attribute specifies the HTTP method that is used to send the data to the server. The various types of METHODs were described earlier in this section. The default is the GET method.

The ENCTYPE specifies how the data can be encoded.

Server Side Includes

Server side includes provide a nonstandard way for the server to include dynamically generated information into an HTML document. The HTML document includes special directives to permit addition of this information. This facility is available in NCSA's Web server as well as in some of the commercially available Web servers. Additional details can be found in other books on the Web such as Ford (1995).

Online Commerce

"Living off the Net: Attempting to do all of your shopping on the Internet is the ultimate virtual lifestyle experiment."

Steven J. Vaughan-Nichols, *Internet World*. June 1995. p. 44

For many businesses, the Internet presents the promise of a virtual marketplace. The Web browser offers the interface to the user, and the Web server provides the storage and processing for store fronts and electronic malls. The concept is intriguing and real; the possibilities stretch our imagination. As of this writing, Internet marketing is becoming pervasive and online commerce is emerging.

The Web is already being put to a variety of uses: educational, social, political, and commercial. Commerce on the Internet is just getting off the ground. The industry is building the infrastructure to securely transact commerce on the Web, while Web servers provide the online malls and store fronts, Computer-related companies are among the first to initiate electronic commerce on the Internet. However, this is just the beginning. There is more to come and it may very well change the way we transact business.

Using various elements of the World Wide Web described in Appendix B, this appendix outlines approaches to accomplish online commerce on the Web. Consider the following sequence for online shopping. John gets up in the morning, powers up his Web browser and downloads some cash on his hard drive. Next he enters the URL of a popular electronic shopping mall. He browses on the mall and finds a TV store that is selling a variety of TV brands. He clicks on that store and gets to the home page of the store. John selects the desired TV, makes the payment, and the TV is now ordered. Let us enumerate these steps.

- Power up the Web browser
- Download cash from the bank account (or charge the credit card)
- Enter the URL for an electronic mall
- Browse the mall and find the desired store
- Click on the highlighted hyperlink (described in Appendix B) for the desired store
- View the home page of the selected store and make the selection for the desired TV
- Click to order the TV, select the desired payment mode, and approve the order
- Log off

The various elements of online commerce are shown in Figure C.1. The Web browser provides the user with access to the Internet. The information on the stores is saved at the Web servers as HTML documents (described in Appendix B).

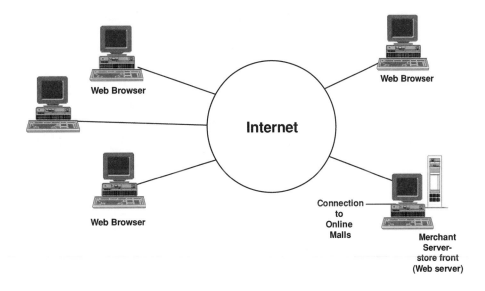

Figure C.1: Online Commerce

As stated, a user usually begins by accessing an online mall. This mall may be stored under a URL at some Web server. The home page of the mall includes a hyperlink for the home page of each store on the mall. Figure C.2 depicts how the electronic mall and online stores work. Figure C.2a shows the user view and Figure C.2b depicts the underlying use of the Web elements on the Internet.

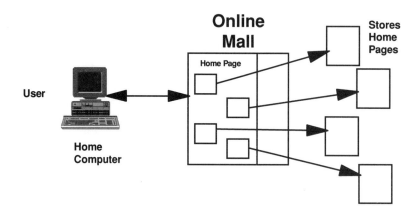

Figure C.2a: User View of Online Commerce

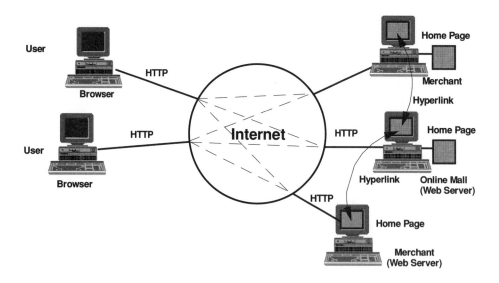

Figure C.2b: Underlying Network for Online Commerce

To set up a store front on the Internet, the merchant first needs to gain access to the Internet. Once connected to the Internet, the merchant must install and configure a Web server. Once the Web server is up, the merchant then must create a home page for the store and save it on the Web server. Finally, the merchant may also wish to be connected to one or more online malls. The connection to an online mall can be provided by including a brief description of the store's products in the mall's home page and providing hyperlinks between the home page of the mall and the store. Note that no changes are required to the Web browsers.

So, the following steps are required for setting up a store front:

1. Establish access to the Internet

2. Create a Web site by installing and configuring a Web server

3. Define a home page and establish a store front on the Web site

4. Define hyperlinks between the home pages of the online malls and the store

Each of these steps is described in greater detail below.

Internet Access

Access to the Internet can be provided in one of three ways. The Internet connection may be through a dial-up connection or direct connection. The dial-up connection provides a *Shell account*. It is easy to install and relatively less expensive. The direct connections entail leased links and are more expensive than the dial-up connections. In terms of features and cost, there is an intermediate level of connection called *SLIP (Serial Line Internet Protocol)* or *PPP (Point-to-Point Protocol)*.

Online services are also offering Internet access. Such access is convenient since you get both the online services as well as access to the Internet. However, I am not aware of any online service also offering the establishment of a Web site and creation of an online home page. For such needs, a direct Internet connection may be the right choice.

Shell Accounts

With a *shell account*, you access the Internet from your home computer through a dial-up connection. The remote host performs actions on the Internet on your behalf. Your keyboard controls the remote host which is usually a UNIX machine. In this connection, your computer is not on the Internet. Instead, you are using the remote host that is on the Internet.

As stated earlier, a shell account is relatively inexpensive. You usually dial through a modem and interact with the remote host through text-based line commands. For example, the remote host will prompt you with a dollar sign or percent sign for the UNIX system. A *shell* is a piece of software on a UNIX system that receives and processes commands from a terminal. Several UNIX shells are available with different formats and functions. Some Internet service providers offer their users a more user-friendly interface. For example, such an interface may prompt you to press 1 for e-mail, 2 for FTP, and so on.

To set up a shell account, you need to have the following:

- Telephone number of the service provider

- Your username and password
- Capability to use your software

SLIP and PPP Access

SLIP (Serial Line Internet Protocol) and *PPP (Point-to-Point Protocol)* permit your machine to run the Internet software. The connection to the Internet is made through a standard phone connection. As such, you can run the FTP client or Mosaic client from your own host. The most important distinction with the shell account is that on a SLIP connection, you do not have to use the command-line interfaces. By using the graphical interfaces, you have easy-to-use access to the Internet services. Instead of entering text commands, you can use the mouse to make selections.

SLIP connections require specialized communications software such as TCP/IP to connect the user host to the Internet. It also requires a 486 PC or higher machine and a 14,400 baud or 28,800 baud modem. To establish a SLIP connection, you will need the following information that is supplied by the Internet service provider.

- Your IP Address: your dotted IP address as described in Appendix B. You will enter the dotted IP address, although some service providers use *dynamic IP addresses*, in which case a different IP address is assigned every time a connection is established.
- Nameserver(s): the IP address of your nameserver.

- Host name: your user ID. For example, in my case, it may be *vahuja* or *vijay*.

- Provider's Domain Name: the service provider's domain name. For example, it may be *xyz.com*, where *xyz* is the company name of the provider.

There are some drawbacks in using SLIP connections:

- SLIP connections require specialized software that may be expensive and must be installed in your host

- Charges for SLIP connections are usually higher than the Shell accounts

- Since SLIP connections often use graphical software, the performance is often slower than the shell accounts.

	Shell	**SLIP/PPP**
Software:	Any communications software	Specialized software
Set up:	Easy to set up	More complexto set up
Cost:	Cheap	More expensive
User Interface:	Text-based	Graphical
Relative Performance:	Fast due to textual interface(depends on the link capacity)	Slow due to graphical interface
Client Software:	Must use provider's client software. No need to install your own.	Choose and install your own client software

Table C.1: Comparison of Shell Account and SLIP/PPP Connection

Dedicated Connection

A dedicated connection designates your host as a full Internet node. Dedicated connections require leased lines; the commonly available speeds are 56 kilobits/s, T1 or T3. A T1 operates at 1.54 megabits/s and a T3 runs at 45 megabits/s. As a full Internet node, you may also require a router to route the Internet traffic that is passing through the node. So, the costs for a dedicated connection include the purchase of a medium-sized host machine, the Web software, the router, and the charges for the leased connection.

Web Site

Once connected to the Internet, the next step is to install and configure a Web server. A Web server is a passive program that listens to requests from the browser and responds to them. These requests are communicated through *Hypertext Transfer Protocol (HTTP)*. Web servers provide a myriad of information to the browser programs. Programs that are invoked by the Web servers are called *gateways*. Information is passed between the server and the gateways through *Common Gateway Interface (CGI)*, described in Appendix B.

The functions of a Web server are:

- Respond to HTTP requests from the browser
- Store and service HTML documents
- Invoke gateways to generate dynamic documents
- Serve as a proxy server, described later

CERN and NCSA developed the two well-known implementations of Web servers. The CERN and the NCSA servers both provide several capabilities. These implementations have in turn provided the basis for many commercial Web products.

The program that runs on the Web server and communicates with the Web browser is called the *Hypertext Transfer Protocol Daemon (HTTPD)*. HTTPD controls the HTTP connection and processes browser requests.

CERN Web Server

The first Web server, the CERN HTTPD, was written by Tim Berners-Lee. CERN HTTPD Version 3.0 was released in September 1994 and is available as freeware. The CERN Web server is well-designed and is the basis of many Web products including those from IBM. It includes support for storing and serving HTML documents and CGI scripts, proxy server, caching access control, request logging, and controlling directory display.

HTML Document and CGI Support

The CERN Web server stores and serves HTML documents. Since it supports CGI, you can also write programs that return customized information for the browser. For example, these programs can process forms and images, perform searches or interact with databases. CERN also provides CGI programs that can process image maps (called *htimage*) or parse CGI input (called *cgiparse*).

Caching Proxy Server

CERN Web servers provide a caching *proxy server*. A proxy server forwards requests and responses between a browser and a server. A proxy server is often used when the browser and the server are in different networks.

A *caching proxy server* can be configured to store the documents that it forwards. Later, these stored documents can be retrieved to respond more quickly to other requests for the same document. A caching proxy server also reduces the network traffic by avoiding access to remote servers with repeated requests for the same documents. For large networks, a hierarchy of caching servers can be created. Requests are forwarded through the hierarchy until the document is obtained from a caching server or the actual server where the document resides.

A proxy server can also be set up on a firewall. Because the firewall provides a barrier between the secured private network and the Internet, the proxy server can process requests and responses through the firewall. The topic of firewall is presented in Chapter 4.

Access Control

You may not want to allow unrestricted access to all the files and programs on the Web server. For example, you may not want to permit everyone to access the CGI program that processes personnel records of your employees. So the CERN server allows access control based on username or IP address. This access control is implemented using one or more of the following files.

- A Password file that controls access by individual users

- A Group file that controls access for a group of users

- An *Access Control List (ACL)* that specifies access rights for each file or group of files

Request Logging

The CERN server provides an option to record the requests that are made to the server. In this way, you can observe and analyze the traffic on your Web server.

Directory Display Control

The CERN Web server can also be configured to control the way in which a directory's information is displayed to the user. This display format may depend on the purpose of the directory and the type of information that is required by the users. In certain cases, it may be important to display the contents of the files along with the list of the filenames. The CERN Web server permits selection of the file information for display, such as:

- The file date

- The file size

- The access control attributes for the file

Installation and Availability

Precompiled versions of the CERN Web server are available on several UNIX operating systems. These systems include: Hewlett Packard HP/UX, Digital Equipment Corporation's Ultrix and OSF/1, Sun Microsystems Solaris and SunOS, IBM RS/6000 with AIX, and Silicon Graphics. If the binary version is available for your Web server, then the installation process is relatively easy. You retrieve the binary version, un-tar the files, and move the program files *httpd*, *htadm*, *htimage*, *cgiparse*, and *cgiutils* to an appropriate directory. If the binary version for your operating system is not available, then you may need the source files. Details for such installation can be found in various books including Ford (1995).

NCSA Web Server

NCSA HTTPD was written by Rob McCool. NCSA HTTPD Version 1.3 was released in May 1994 and is available in the public domain. It has functions similar to the CERN Web server. For example, both servers support resource mapping and request logging. In the following description of the NCSA Web server, we include some of the distinctions between the NCSA Web server and the CERN Web server.

CGI Support

NCSA Web server supports CGI so users can write programs that process requests from the browser. In addition, the NCSA Web server also provides several sample CGI programs including the following:

- A CGI program, *archie*, that provides interface to the Internet search tool archie described in Appendix B. This tool searches anonymous FTP servers for files that match the specified selection criteria.

- A CGI program from NCSA, *date*, that displays the current date.

- A CGI program, *query*, that creates a generic form response.

Access Control

The NCSA Web server also provides the capability to restrict access to the files residing at the server. The access control can be exercised based on the *host name* or the *username*.

The access control by host name permits access to only those users that are on specific host systems. For example, you may restrict some of the files to be accessible to only the users in your company by specifying the host name of each machine within your company.

The files at the Web server can also be controlled by the user-name. This access control requires users or user groups to authenticate themselves. Each defined user is assigned a pass-word and the user must enter his or her password to access cer-tain files. The password file can be maintained through the use of *htpasswd* command.

Installation and Availability

As with the CERN Web server, compiled versions of NCSA's Web server are available for most UNIX operating systems, including Digital Equipment Corporation Alpha and Ultrix, Hewlett Packard HP/UX, IBM RS/6000, SUN Microsystems SunOS, and Silicon Graphics. The compiled code of NCSA Web server can be found at:
http://hoohoo.ncsa.uiuc.edu/docs/setup/PreCompiled.html.

Details on NCSA's HTTPD can be found at:
http://hoohoo.ncsa.uiuc.edu/docs/Overview.html. As of this writing, the current release of NCSA Web server is HTTPd 1.5c. HTTPd Release 1.5 supports several authentication schemes including MD5, and Kerberos Versions 4 and 5. This release also has fea-tures to support access control.

Besides the two freeware Web servers from CERN and NCSA, several commercial versions of Web products are also available from software vendors such as Netscape and IBM.

Additional details on Web servers can be found in several books such as Ford (1995), Kantor (1995), Ellsworth (1994), Mathiesen (1995), and Morrison (1995). LeVitus (1996b) provides a detailed description on building a World Wide Web server including the software to install the Web server on a Windows operating system. Kwan (1995) provides an in-depth review of the design and performance of the NCSA Web server.

Home Page

A *home page* typically presents a short outline about a business or an institution. Several businesses have already established their home page on the Internet. The home page is written in HTML and stored in the Web server. Although learning HTML is relatively easy and very helpful, software vendors are rolling out products to convert documents in other formats to HTML. The rules for writing in HTML were presented in Appendix B. Some important aspects for a home page are listed below.

- Provide navigation aids: Users often surf the Internet by navigating through several home pages. It is useful to provide linkages to go backward to the previous document and to go forward to retrieve a document of interest. Usually, there are several forward links that provide access to related documents. If your document is large, then you may also provide links between the beginning and the end of the document.

- Include useful notation for links: The following example illustrates the different ways to describe links. Consider the statement:

  "For additional information, contact your local Post Office."

  This statement indicates that to obtain more information, you can contact the local post office. It also implies that by clicking here, you can see more information about the *local Post Office*. On the contrary, the following statement does not demonstrate a good use of the linkage statements.

  "For additional information, click here."

  This statement does not indicate the kind of home page that will be retrieved through this hyperlink.

- Use complete headings and avoid copying other documents.

- Add graphics, images, video, and sound to make the home pages more attractive and easier to communicate with the user. However, home pages with several graphic images are slow to retrieve for a typical home user with 14.4 kilobits/s or 28.8 kilobits/s modem.

The home page can also be used to provide a live demo of your products. By using tools that employ animation, the home page can demonstrate the use and benefits of your products.

Establishing a Store Front

Establishing a home page on the Web server simply provides access to information about your products or business. To provide a store front and transact commerce, your Web site must include more functions than those of the Web server presented earlier. The additional functions include processing transactions, displaying product features and prices, managing catalog and inventory, and interfacing to the traditional merchant system.

Merchant Server

A *merchant server* permits a business to transact commerce over the Web. Figure C.3 depicts a hypothetical merchant server residing on a Web server.

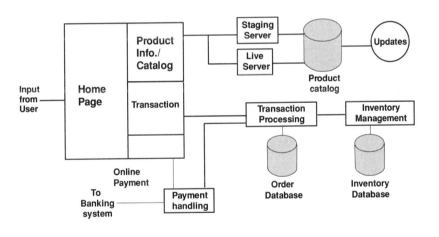

Figure C.3: A Hypothetical Online Merchant System

A merchant system includes the following four major types of functions: transaction processing, catalog management, payment handling, and inventory management.

There are probably other functions of a merchant server that are not addressed here. Additional details including the marketing aspects of merchant server can be found in other books such as Ellsworth (1994) and Mathiesen (1995).

Transaction Processing

Transaction processing handles the customer orders or inquiries. It in turn initiates actions to process the order and shipment of the purchased item. It also updates the inventory system to flag the sold item and updates the quantity of goods available for sale. Transaction processing handles customer inquiries by determining the status of customer orders.

Catalog Management

The product descriptions and the current prices are constantly updated and displayed as part of the product catalog. The *staging server* provides the capability to test the system with updates to the home page or product catalog. Typically, the product information is stored in a database on the Web server and is displayed on the Web browser.

Payment Handling

Payment handling requires secure exchange of information among the user, the merchant, and the bank or the credit card company. Most of the payment information should be protected from hackers. This information includes the credit card number and the expiration date. It may also include the permission to transfer a certain amount of money from the user's account to the merchant's account. The topic of secure payment schemes is addressed in Chapter 8.

Inventory Management

Inventory management programs can operate as a background process to track the available quantities of various products. The user on the Web browser is not directly exposed to a store's inventory. However, inventory management responds to user inquiries on whether the desired quantities of goods are available for sale.

Linkage to Online Malls

To market and sell its products, an online store has to gain visibility to the users on the Web browsers. This is perhaps one of the most important uses of hyperlinks for merchant systems. Hyperlinks allow the user to view a chain of related information spread across the Internet by simply clicking a mouse button. As an illustration, I started from the home page of the Internet Society and, working through a chain of links, I accessed the Internet RFCs.

To begin, the merchant should identify the online malls that are frequently visited by the users interested in the merchant's line of products. Next, the store has to establish presence in the selected malls and provide its product description. It is often prudent to be enlisted in more than one mall. In addition, the store should also have its own URL to allow direct access from a Web user to the store's merchant server. Figure C.4 shows a simple overview of linking the various documents of the malls and stores.

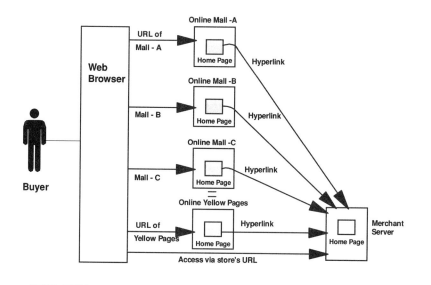

Figure C.4: Linkages to Access a Merchant's Storefront

Various malls are emerging on the Internet. Information on these malls can be obtained from Internet literature and the trade press.

Finally, let me narrate a personal experience as an example. I found the URL for an online mall, *Access Market Square*, from a trade journal. The URL is:

http://www.icw.com/ams.html

Upon accessing this mall, there was a graphical display of the mall that depicted stores for arts & crafts, food court, clothing, services, specialty shops, sports products, and so on. By clicking on one of these, I obtained more information about the merchandise for the selected type of stores. The home page also presented a thank-you message such as *Thanks for dropping in*. In addition, it provided me the option to view *What's new* and the *last update*.

Bibliography

[Abrams 1990] Marshall D. Abrams, Leonard J. La Padula, and Ingrid M. Olson, "Building Generalized Access Control on UNIX," Proceedings of UNIX Security Workshop. USENIX Association. August 27–28, 1990. Portland, OR.

[Ahuja 1996] Vijay Ahuja, "Network and Internet Security," AP Professional. 1996.

[Ahuja 1982] Vijay Ahuja, "Design and Analysis of Computer Communication Networks," McGraw-Hill Book Company. 1982.

[Amoroso 1994] Edward G. Amoroso, "Fundamentals of Computer Security Technology," Prentice Hall, Inc. 1994.

[Anthes 1995] Gary H. Anthes, "Hackers Try New Tacks," Computerworld. January 30, 1995. p. 12.

[Atkinson 1995a] R. Atkinson, "Security Architecture for the Internet Protocol," RFC 1825. August 1995.

[Atkinson 1995b] R. Atkinson, "IP Authentication Header," RFC 1826. August 1995.

[Atkinson 1995c] R. Atkinson, "IP Encapsulation Security Payload (ESP)," RFC 1827. August 1995.

[Balenson 1993] D. Balenson, "Privacy Enhancement for Internet Electronic Mail: Part III Algorithms, Modes, and Identifiers," RFC 1423. February 1993.

[Bakel 1996] Rogier Van Bakel, "The Check is in the E-Mail," NetGuide. April 1996. pp. 68-76.

[Baran 1990] Fuat Baran, Howard Kaye, and Margarita Suarez, "Security Breaches: Five Recent Incidents at Columbia University," UNIX Security Workshop. USENIX Association. August 27–28, 1990. pp. 151–167.

[Barlow 1993] John Perry Barlow, "A Plain Text on Crypto Policy," Communications of the ACM. Vol. 36. No. 11. November 1993. pp. 21–26.

[Bellare 1995] Mihir Bellare, Juan A. Garay, Ralf Hauser, Amir Herzberg, Hugo Krawczyk, Michael Steiner, Gene Tsudik, and Michael Waidner, "iKP—A Family of Secure Electronic Payment Protocols," Extended Abstract. USENIX Workshop on Electronic Commerce. July 11–12, 1995. New York, NY.

[Benaloh 1995] Josh Benaloh, Butler Lampson, Daniel Simon, Terence Spies, and Bennet Yee, "Private Communication Technology Protocol," Internet Draft. September 1995.

[Berners-Lee 1995] T. Berners-Lee and D. Connolly, "Hypertext Markup Language—2.0," RFC 1866. November 1995.

[Berners-Lee 1996] T. Berners-Lee, R. Fielding, H. Frystyk, "Hypertext Transfer Protocol—HTTP/1.0," Internet-Draft. February 19, 1996. Expires August 19, 1996. Section 3.2.1.

[Bishop 1992] Matt Bishop, "Anatomy of a Proactive Password Changer," UNIX Security Symposium. USENIX Association. Baltimore, MD. September 14–16, 1992. pp. 171–184.

[Bishop 1990] Matt Bishop, "An Extendable Password Checker," Extended Abstract. UNIX Security Workshop. USENIX Association. Portland, OR. August 27–28, 1990. pp. 15–16.

[Bournellis 1995] Cynthia Bournellis, "Internet'95," Internet World. November 1995. pp. 47–52.

[Brown 1984] P. J. Brown, "Starting with UNIX," Addison-Wesley Publishing Company. 1984.

[Brown 1994] Patricia Brown, "ICL Extends AccessManager to Sun Platforms," Communications Week. October 17, 1994. p. 4.

[Browne 1995] R. Browne, "Extended Abstract: An Architecture for Covert Channel Control in RealTime Networks and MultiProcessors," IEEE Symposium on Security and Privacy. Oakland, CA. May 8–10, 1995. pp. 155–168.

[Busch 1996] David P. Busch, "Image Is Everything," NetGuide, March 1996. pp. 56–69.

[Butler 1994] Mark Butler, "How to Use the Internet," Ziff-Davis Press. 1994.

[Caldwell 1995] Bruce Caldwell, "Hacking Spree Targets Citibank," InformationWeek. September 4, 1995. p. 20.

[Carlin 1993] Jerry M. Carlin, "UNIX (R) Security Update," UNIX Security Symposium IV, USENIX Association. Santa Clara, CA. October 4–6, 1993. pp. 119–130.

[Carson 1998] Mark E. Carson and Wen-Der Jiang, "New Ideas in Discretionary Access Control," UNIX Security Workshop, USENIX Association. Portland, OR. August 27–28, 1988. pp. 35–37.

[CERT 1995] CERT Advisory, "Security Administrator Tool for Analyzing Networks," CA-95:06. April 3, 1995.

[CERTB 1995] "Today's Challenge," CERT Brochure. CERT Coordination Center, Software Engineering Institute, Carnegie Mellon University. Pittsburgh, PA. 15213-3890. CONTACT: cert @ cert.org

[CERTFAQ 1993] CERT, "The CERT Coordination Center FAQ," Revision 7. JPO#93-025 and ESC#93-0115. cert.org:/pub/cert_advisories/01-README January 1993.

[Chapman 1995] D. Brent Chapman and Elizabeth D. Zwicky, "Building Internet Firewalls," O'Reilly & Associates, Inc. 1995.

[Cheswick 1994] William R. Cheswick and Steven M. Bellovin, "Firewalls and Internet Security: Repelling the Wily Hacker," Addison-Wesley Publishing Company. 1994.

[Chokhani 1992] Santosh Chokhani, "Trusted Products Evaluation," Communications of the ACM. Vol. 35. No. 7. July 1992. pp. 65–76.

[Churbuck 1995] David C. Churbuck, "Where's the Money?," Forbes. January 30, 1995. pp. 100–108.

[Clark 1991] "Computers at Risk," David D. Clark, Chairman. System Security Study Committee, Computer Science and Telecommunications Board. Commission on Physical Sciences, Mathematics, and Applications. National Research Council. National Academy Press. 1991.

[Cobb 1996] Sephen Cobb, "Containing the New Macro Viruses," Internetwork. April 1996. p. 16.

[Comer 1991] Douglas E. Comer, "Internetworking with TCP/IP. Volume I. Principles, Protocols and Architecture," Prentice-Hall. 1991.

[Curry 1992] David A. Curry, "UNIX(R) System Security: A Guide for Users and System Administrators," Addison-Wesley Publishing Co., Inc. 1992.

[De Alvare' 1990] Ana Maria De Alvare', "How Crackers Crack Passwords or What Passwords to Avoid," UNIX Security Workshop. USENIX Association. Portland, OR. August 27–28. 1990. pp. 103–112.

[Denning 1996] Dorothy E. Denning and Dennis K. Branstad, "A Taxonomy for Key Escrow Encryption Systems," Communications of the ACM. March 1996. Vo. 39. No. 3. pp. 34–40.

[Denning 1987] Dorothy E. Denning, "An Intrusion-Detection Model," IEEE Transactions on Software Engineering. Vol. SE-13. No. 2. February 1987. pp. 222–232.

[Diffie 1976] Whitfield Diffie and Martin E. Hellman, "New Directions in Cryptography," IEEE Transactions on Information Theory. Vol. IT-22. No. 6. November 1976. pp. 644–654.

[Dunlap 1995] Charlotte Dunlap, "Netscape to Enter New Turf: Web Site Development Tools," Computer Reseller News. September 11, 1995. p. 12.

[Eastlake 1996] D. Eastlake 3rd, B. Boesch, S. Crocker, and M. Yesil, "CyberCash Credit Card Protocol Version 0.8," RFC 1898. February 1996.

[Edwards 1993] John Edwards, "Single Sign-on Technology Streamlines Network Access," Software Magazine. Client/Server Computing Special Edition. November 1993. pp. 35–42.

[Ellsworth 1994] Jill H. Ellsworth and Matthew V. Ellsworth, "The Internet Business Book," John Wiley & Sons, Inc. 1994.

[Ellsworth 1995] Jill H. Ellsworth, "Boom Town," Internet World. June 1995. pp. 33–36.

[Ford 1995] Andrew Ford, "Spinning the Web: How to Provide Information on the Internet," VNR International Thomson Publishing Company. 1995.

[FSTC 1994] "The Challenge—The Response," Financial Services Technology Consortium Handout. September 23, 1994.

[Galvin 1993] J. Galvin and K. McCloghrie, "Security Protocols for Version 2 of the Simple Network Management Protocol (SNMPv2)," RFC 1446. April 1993.

[Ganesan 1996] Ravi Ganesan, "The Yaksha Security System," Communications of the ACM. March 1996. Vol. 39. No. 3. pp.55–59.

[Girling 1987] C. Gray Girling, "Covert Channels in LAN's," IEEE Transactions on Software Engineering. Vol. SE-13. No. 2. February 1987. pp. 292–296.

[Hickman 1995] Kipp E. B. Hickman and Taher Elgamal, "The SSL Protocol," Internet Draft. June 1995.

[Hurwicz 1995] Mike Hurwicz, "Under Lock and Key," Special Report. LAN Magazine. March 1995. pp. 116–121.

[Hwang 1995] Diana Hwang and Ken Yamada, "Resellers Reap High Margins, Steady Business from the Internet," Computer Reseller News. August 14, 1995. p. 3.

[IBMAIX 1994] "Distributed Computing Environment 1.3 for AIX: Release Notes," IBM Corporation. GC23-2434-02. October 1994.

[IBMAIXS 1991] IBM Corporation, "Elements of AIX Security: R3.1," GG24-3622-01. April 1991.

[IBMDATAS 1977] "Data Security through Cryptography," IBM Corporation. GC22-9062-0. October 1977.

[IBMDSM 1995] "Distributed Security Manager for MVS," IBM Corporation. 1994. G221-4236-00.

[IBMEWS 1995] "Enterprise-Wide Security Architecture and Solutions Presentation Guide," IBM Corporation. SG24-4579-00. November 1995.

[IBMFW 1995] "Building a Firewall with the NetSP Secured Network Gateway," IBM Corporation. GG24-2577-00. April 1995.

[IBMRACF 1993] "Resource Access Control Facility: Secured Signon SPE Information Package Version 1 Release 9.2," IBM Corporation. SC23-3765-00. September 1993.

[IBMSEC 1995] "IBM Security Architecture—Securing the Open Client/ Server Distributed Enterprise," IBM Corporation. SC28-8135-01. June 1995.

[IBMSLC 1994] "Network Security Program Product Guide Version 1 Release 2," IBM Corporation. SC31-6500-01. July 1994.

[IBMTCP 1990] "TCP/IP Tutorial and Technical Overview," IBM Corporation. June 1990. GG24-3376-01.

[INFOWEEK 1995] "Virus Count Up Sharply," Information Week. May 15, 1995. p. 12.

[InfoSec 1994] "Securing the Infobahn," InfoSecurity Newsletter. July/August 1994.

[ISS 1996] "Internet Scanner 3.2," Internet Security Systems. 1996.

[ITSEC 1991] "Information Technology Security Evaluation Criteria (ITSEC)," Version 1.2. Office for Official Publications of the European Communities. Luxemburg. 1991.

[Johnson 1994] D. B. Johnson, S. M. Matyas, A. V. Le, and J. D. Wilkins, "The Commercial Data Masking Facility (CDMF) Data Privacy Algorithm," IBM Journal of Research and Development. Vol. 38. No. 2. March 1994. pp. 217–226.

[Johnson 1995] Johna Till Johnson and Kevin Tolly, "Token Authentication: The Safety Catch," Data Communication. May 1995. pp. 62–77.

[Jolitz 1995] William F. Jolitz and Lynne Greer Jolitz, "Internet Security Breach," Dr. Dobb's Developer Update. Vol 2. No. 3. March 1995. pp. 3-4.

[Kahn 1971] Robert E. Kahn and William R. Krother, "A Study of the ARPA Network Design and Performance," Bolt Beranek and Newman, Inc. Report No. 2161. August 1971.

[Kaliski 1993] B. Kaliski, "Privacy Enhancement for Internet Electronic Mail: Part IV. Key Certification and Related Services," RFC 1424. February 1993.

[Kang 1995] M. H. Kang, I. S. Moskowitz and D. C. Lee, "A Network Version of the Pump," IEEE Symposium on Security and Privacy. Oakland, CA. May 8–10, 1995. pp. 144–154.

[Kantor 1995] Andrew Kantor, "Mecklermedia's Official Internet World™—60 Minute Guide to the Internet including the World-Wide Web," IDG Books Worldwide, Inc. 1995.

[Karn 1995] P. Karn, P. Metzger and W. Simpson, "The ESP DES-CBC Transform," RFC 1829. August 1995.

[Kaufman 1995] Charlie Kaufman, Radia Perlman and Mike Speciner, "Network Security—PRIVATE Communication in a PUBLIC World," Prentice Hall. 1995. p. 17.

[Kemmerer 1983] Richard A. Kemmerer, "Shared Resource Matrix Methodology: An Approach to Identifying Storage and Timing Channels," ACM Transactions on Computer Systems, Vol. 1, No. 3, August 1983, pp. 256–277.

[Kent 1993a] S. Kent, "Privacy Enhancement for Internet Electronic Mail: Part II Certificate-Based Key Management," RFC 1422. February 1993.

[Kent 1993b] Stephen T. Kent, "Internet Privacy Enhanced Mail," Communications of the ACM, August 1993. Vol. 36. No. 8. pp. 48–59.

[Khare 1996] Rohit Khare, "PEP: An Extension Mechanism for HTTP/1.1," W3C Working Draft. February 20, 1996.

[Klein 1990] Daniel V. Klein, "Foiling the Cracker: A Survey of, and Improvements to, Password Security". UNIX Security Workshop. USENIX Association. Portland, OR. August 27–28, 1990.

[Koblas 1992] David Koblas and Michelle R. Koblas, "SOCKS", Proceedings of UNIX Security Symposium. USENIX Association. Baltimore, MD. September 14–16, 1992. pp. 77–82.

[Kocher 1995] Paul C. Kocher, "Cryptanalysis of Diffie-Hellman, RSA, DSS, and Other Systems Using Timin Attacks," Extended Abstract. December 7, 1995.

[Kohl 1993] J. Kohl and B. Neuman, "The Kerberos Network Authentication Service (V5)," RFC 1510. September 10, 1993.

[Kohlhepp 1996] Robert J. Kohllepp, "InterScan Blocks Internet Viruses," Network Computing. February 15, 1996. pp. 46–52.

[Kwan 1995] Thomas T. Kwan and Robert E. McGrath, "NCSA's World Wide Web Server: Design and Performance," IEEE Computer. November 1995. pp. 68–74.

[Leech 1994] Marcus Leech, "SOCKS Protocol Version 4." Internet-Draft. Exp. December 1994.

[LeVitus 1996a] Bob LeVitus and Jeff Evans, "WebMaster Macintosh," AP Professional. 1996.

[LeVitus 1996b] Bob LeVitus and Jeff Evans, "WebMaster Windows," AP Professional. 1996.

[Linn 1993a] J. Linn, "Privacy Enhancement for Internet Electronic Mail: Part I Message Encryption and Authentication Procedures," RFC 1421. February 1993.

[Linn 1993b] J. Linn, "Generic Security Service Application Program Interface," RFC 1508. September 1993.

[Lockhart 1994] Harold W. Lockhart, Jr., "OSF DCE: Guide to Developing Distributed Applications," McGraw-Hill, Inc. 1994.

[Loeb 1996] Larry Loeb, "The Stage is SET," Internet World. August 1996. pp. 55–59.

[Loepere 1985] Keith Loepere, "Resolving Covert Channels within a B2 Class Secure System," ACM Operating System Review. Vol 19. No. 3. July 1985. pp. 9–28.

[Loshin 1995] Pete Loshin, "Electronic Commerce—On-Line Ordering and Digital Money," Charles River Media, Inc. 1995.

[Ludwig 1990] Mark A. Ludwig, "The Little Black Book of Computer Viruses," American Eagle Publications, Inc. 1990.

[Lunt 1990] Steven J. Lunt, "Experiences with Kerberos," UNIX Security Workshop. USENIX Association. Portland, OR. August 27–28, 1990. pp. 113–120.

[Lynch 1996] Daniel C. Lynch and Leslie Lundquist, "Digital Money—The New Era of Internet Commerce," John Wiley & Sons, Inc. 1996. p. 96.

[Maddox 1995] Kate Maddox, Mitch Wagner, and Clinton Wilder, "Making Money on the Web," InformationWeek. September 4, 1995. pp. 31–40.

[Maddox 1996] Kate Maddox and Clinton Wilder, "Net Liability," InformationWeek. January 8, 1996. pp.14–16.

[Maher 1996] David Paul Maher, "Crypto Backup and Key Escrow," Communications of the ACM. March 1996. Vol. 39. No. 3. pp. 48–53.

[MarkTwain 1995] "Mark Twain Bank Launches Ecash," Press Release. DigiCash New York. October 23, 1995.

[Marshall 1995] Steve Marshall, "High-Tech Crooks Crack Internet Security," USA Today. January 24, 1995. p. 1A.

[Mathiesen 1995] Michael Mathiesen, "Marketing on the Internet," Maximum Press. 1995.

[MCVISA 1996] "Secure Electronic Transaction (SET) Specification. Book 1: Business Description. Draft for Public Comment," MasterCard Visa. February 23, 1996.

[Metzger 1995] P. Metzger and W. Simpson, "IP Authentication Using Keyed MD5," RFC 1828. August 1995.

[Miller 1967] Benjamin F. Miller, M.D., "The Complete Medical Guide," Simon and Schuster. New York. 1967.

[Morris 1979] Robert Morris and Ken Thompson, "Password Security: A Case History," Communications of the ACM. Vol. 22, No. 11. November 1979. pp. 594–597.

[Morrison 1995] Deborah Morrison, "IBM's Official Guide to Building a Better Web Site," IDG Books Worldwide, Inc. 1995.

[Needham 1994] Roger M. Needham, "Denial of Service: An Example," Communications of the ACM. November 1994. Vol 37. No 11. pp. 42–46.

[Needham 1978] Roger M. Needham and Michael D. Schroeder, "Using Encryption for Authentication in Large Networks of Computers," Communications of the ACM. Vol. 21. No. 12. December 1978. pp. 993–999.

[Neumann 1996] Peter Neumann, "Risks in Digital Commerce," Communications of the ACM. January 1996. Vol. 39. No. 1. p. 154.

[Obermayer 1996] Joel B. Obermayer, "Banking' Frontier: Cyberspace," The Sunday News & Observer. January 21, 1996. p. 1A.

[OSF 1990] "OSF Distributed Computing Environment Rationale," Open Software Foundation. May 14, 1990.

[OSFDCE11 1995] "OSF DCE 1.1 New Features," Open Software Foundation. OSF-DCE-DS-195. 1995.

[OST 1993] "In New York City Break-In, An Echo of '88 Worm Attack," Open Systems Today. November 8, 1993. p. 19.

[OpenVision 1994] "OpenVision Today," OpenVision Technologies, Inc. June 1994.

[Panurach 1996] Patiwat Panurach, "Money in Electronic Commerce: Digital Cash, Electronic Fund Transfer, and Ecash," Communications of the ACM. June 1996. pp. 45–50.

[Phillips 1995a] Ken Phillips, "Virus Whistleblowers," PCWEEK September 18, 1995. pp. N1–N10.

[Phillips 1995b] Ken Phillips, "What Makes Anti-Virus Sleuth Engines Hum," PCWEEK September 18, 1995. pages N1-N15.

[Pounds 1995] Stephen Pounds, "The Latest Techno-bump on the Information Superhighway is how to keep hackers out of your Computer—and away from your Wallet," Palm Beach Post. March 12, 1995. p. 1E.

[Press 1994] Larry Press, "Commercialization of the Internet," Communications of the ACM. November 1994. Vol. 37. No. 11. pp.17–21.

[Ragett 1996] Dave Ragett, "The HTML3 Table Model," W3C Working Draft. January 23, 1996.

[Raleigh 1988] T. M. Raleigh and R. W. Underwood, "CRACK: A Distributed Password Advisor," Abstract. UNIX Security Workshop. USENIX Association. Portland, OR. August 29–30, 1988.

[Rescorla 1995] E. Rescorla and A. Schiffman, "The Secure HyperText Transfer Protocol," Internet Draft. July 1995.

[Rivest 1978] R. L. Rivest, A. Shamir, and L. Adleman, "A Method for Obtaining Digital Signatures and Public-Key Cryptosystems," Communications of the ACM. February 1978. Vol. 21. No. 2. pp. 120–126.

[Rivest 1992a] R. Rivest, "The MD5 Message-Digest Algorithm," RFC 1321. April 1992.

[Rivest 1992b] R. Rivest, "The MD4 Message-Digest Algorithm," RFC 1320. April 1992.

[Rosenberry 1992] Ward Rosenberry, David Kenney, and Gerry Fisher, "OSF Distributed Computing Environment: Understanding DCE," O'Reilly & Associates, Inc. 1992.

[Rosenthal 1995] D. Rosenthal, "Use of the GSS-API for Web Security," Internet Draft. November 1995.

[RSA 1993] "Answers to Frequently Asked Questions About Today's Cryptography," RSA Laboratories. Revision 2.0. October 1993.

[Russell 1991] Deborah Russell and G. T. Gangemi Sr., "Computer Security Basics," O'Reilly & Associates, Inc. 1991.

[Salamone 1993] Salvatore Salamone, "Internetwork Security: Unsafe at Any Node?," Data Communications. September 1993. pp. 61–68.

[Schatz 1995] Willie Schatz, "The Secret to Encryption," InformationWeek. May 15. 1995. pp. 74–76.

[Schneier 1995] Bruce Schneier, "E-Mail Security: How to Keep Your Electronic Messages Private," John Wiley & Sons, Inc. 1995.

[Schneier 1994] Bruce Schneier, "Applied Cryptography: Protocols, Algorithms and Source Code in C," John Wiley & Sons, Inc. 1994.

[Schuman 1993] Evan Schuman, "Robert Morris in 1993: A Portrait of the Cracker as a Less Young Man," Open System Today. November 8, 1993. p. 17.

[Shaffer 1994] Steven L. Shaffer and Alan R. Simon, "Network Security," AP Professional. 1994.

[Simmons 1994] Gustavus J. Simmons, "Cryptanalysis and Protocol Failures," Communications of the ACM. Vol. 37. No. 11. November 1994. pp. 56–65.

[Sinha 1992] Alok Sinha, "Client-Server Computing," Communications of the ACM. July 1992. Vol 35. No. 7. pp. 77–98.

[Siyan 1995] Karanjit Siyan and Chris Hare, "Internet Firewalls and Network Security," New Riders Publishing. 1995.

[Spafford 1992] Eugene H. Spafford, "Observing Reusable Password Choices," UNIX Security Symposium. USENIX Association. Baltimore, MD. September 14–16, 1992. pp. 299–312.

[Stallings 1995] William Stallings, "Network and Internetwork Security: Principles and Practice," Prentice-Hall, Inc. 1995. p.110.

[Stallings 1994] William Stallings, "Kerberos Keeps the Enterprise Secure," Data Communications. October 1994. pp. 103-11.

[Stallings 1990] William Stallings, "Local Networks," MacMillan Publishing Company. New York. 1990.

[Steiner 1988] Jennifer G. Steiner, Clifford Neuman, and Jeffrey I. Schiller, "Kerberos: An Authentication Service for Open Network Systems," Proceedings of the Winter 1988 USENIX Conference. February 1988.

[Stoll 1989] Cliff Stoll, "The Cuckoo's Egg—Tracking a Spy through the Maze of Computer Espionage," Pocket Books, Simon and Schuster, Inc. 1990.

[Strack 1990] Hermann Strack, "Extended Access Control in UNIX System V—ACLs and Context *)", UNIX Security Workshop, USENIX Association. Portland, OR. August 27–28, 1990. pp. 87–101.

[Suggs 1992] Darrell Suggs, "Secure Superuser Access via the Internet,"
Proceedings of UNIX Security Symposium. USENIX Association. September
14–16, 1992. Baltimore, MD.

[Sullivan 1993] Kristina B. Sullivan, "Outwitting Smart Viruses," PC Week,
December 27, 1993/January 3, 1994. Buyer's Guide. p. 81.

[Sullivan 1995] Kristina B. Sullivan, "Protecting Windows 95 from Attack," PC
Week. September 1995. p. N17.

[Surkan 1996] Michael Surkan, "Daemons Defy Hackers," PC Week. February
5, 1996.

[Tardo 1990] Joe Tardo, Kannan Alagappan, and Richard Pitkin, "Public Key
based Authentication Using Internet Certificates," UNIX Security Workshop.
USENIX Association. Portland, OR. August 27–28, 1990. pp. 121–123.

[Thompson 1984] Ken Thompson, "Reflections on Trusting Trust,"
Communications of the ACM. Vol. 27. No. 8. August 1984. pp. 761–763.

[Trident 1996] Brochure by Trident Data Systems. San Antonio, TX 78213.
1996.

[Tsudik 1992] Gene Tsudik, "Message Authentication with One-Way Hash
Functions," INFOCOMM 1992.

[Vaughan-Nichols 1995] Steven J. Vaughan-Nichols, "Living Off the Net,"
Internet World. June 1995. pp. 44–47.

[Violino 1996] Bob Violino, "Word Macro Viruses to Cost Companies Billions
of Dollars," InformationWeek. April 1, 1996. p. 22.

[Wagner 1993] Mitch Wagner, "Possibilities are Endless, and Frightening,"
Open Systems Today. November 8, 1993. pp. 16–19.

[Walker 1996] Stephen T. Walker, Steven B. Lipner, Carl M. Ellson, and David M. Balenson, "Commercial Key Recovery," Communications of the ACM. March 1996. Vol. 39. No. 3. pp. 41–47.

[Wayner 1996] Peter Wayner, "Digital Cash: Commerce on the Net," AP Professional. 1996.

[Welz 1995] Gary Welz, "New Deals," Internet World. June 1995. pp. 36–41.

[Wichers 1990] David R. Wichers, Douglas M. Cook, Ronald A. Olsson, John Crossley, Paul Kerchen, Karl N. Levitt, and Raymond Lo, "PACL's: An Access Control List Approach to Anti-Viral Security," UNIX Security Workshop. Portland, OR. August 27–28, 1990. pp. 71–82.

[Wiggins 1995] Richard W. Wiggins, "Webolution—The Evolution of Revolutionary World-Wide Web, "Internet World. April 1995. pp. 33–38.

[Wilder 1995] Clinton Wilder, Katherine Bull, and Caryn Gillooly, "Intranet Tools," InformationWeek. November 6, 1995. pp. 14–16.

[Winkler 1996] Ira S. Winkler, "Case Study of Industrial Espionage Through Social Engineering," Proceedings of 1996 ISSA Conference. April 1996. pp. 25–31.

[Wood 1995] Brad Wood, "For Your Amusement", May 05, 1995.

[Woolf 1977] Henry Bosley Woolf, Editor-in-Chief,"Webster's New Collegiate Dictionary". G. & C. Merriam Company, Springfield, MA. 1977.

[Wray 1993] J. Wray, "Generic Security Service API: C-bindings," RFC 1509. September 1993.

[Zimmerman 1995] Philip R. Zimmerman, "PGP Source Code and Internals," The MIT Press. 1995.

Index